John L. O'Donnell is a Barrister and a graduate of University College, Dublin, and Cambridge University. He is a Lecturer in the Honourable Society of Kings Inns, and has had numerous articles published in a variety of legal periodicals and journals.

EXAMINERSHIPS

THE COMPANIES (AMENDMENT) ACT, 1990

John L. O'Donnell

WITH A FOREWORD BY

The Hon. Mr Justice Thomas A. Finlay
CHIEF JUSTICE

OAK TREE PRESS

DUBLIN

This book was typeset by
Gilbert Gough Typesetting for
Oak Tree Press, 4 Arran Quay, Dublin 7.

© 1994 John L. O'Donnell

A catalogue number for this book
is available from the British Library.

ISBN 1-872853-25-0 (pbk)
ISBN 1-872853-26-9 (hbk)

For my parents

Printed in Ireland by
Colour Books Ltd

Table of Contents

Foreword

The introduction of the concept of examinership into the statutory company law of Ireland by the enactment of the Companies (Amendment) Act 1990, in the summer of that year, was a timely legislative intervention.

This book by Mr. O'Donnell on the concept of examinership and, in particular, on the provisions of that Act, is a timely book.

In the ordinary way it may well be wise to await a number of years after the passing of a piece of major legislation with legal significance before attempting to write a textbook on it.

In this instance I am clearly of the opinion that an early book was a desirable and necessary task to be undertaken, and I believe that the legal profession and the courts would be correct in feeling themselves indebted to Mr. O'Donnell for his having undertaken that task.

The concept of examinership has, of course, many superficial similarities to the concept of the liquidation of companies and the appointment of receivers over companies, which has been long enshrined in our statute law, and the consequences of which are well known to businessmen as well as to lawyers.

The difference between an examinership and a liquidation or the appointment of a receiver are so fundamental and so far-reaching that it was, in my view, very clearly desirable that a book should have been written with as little delay as possible, underlining and analysing in a clear fashion those differences as well as those similarities. This, in my view, Mr. O'Donnell has very successfully, indeed, achieved, and the courts as well as the legal profession will welcome this book.

The interpretation of the provisions of the Act and, even more importantly, the principles in accordance with which those provisions should be applied have only come before our courts on a relatively limited number of occasions in the last three years. The task of analysing the statute and, in a sense, foreseeing or predicting the principles in accordance with which it should be applied, which has been courageously undertaken by the author in this book has, however, been assisted by his research into the decisions in England on their Insolvency Act of 1986, the provisions of which in many respects are similar to those of our Act of 1990.

The book is short, a virtue rather than a failing in any textbook and, in particular, in a modern legal textbook. It loses nothing by its brevity and appears to me, on a perusal of its contents, to be well assembled, carefully annotated and very clearly expressed. I wish it the success which I believe it deserves.

Thomas A. Finlay
Chief Justice

The Supreme Court
Four Courts
Dublin 7

Preface

The enactment of the Companies (Amendment) Act 1990 was principally a response to the effect of the Iraqi invasion of Kuwait on the Goodman group of companies. The crisis caused by the loss of this sales outlet to the already beleaguered meat industry in Ireland meant that the group required a moratorium from its creditors to avoid collapse. Galvanised into action, the Oireachtas enacted within days Part IX of the Companies (No. 2) Bill of 1987. The effect of the legislation is to allow troubled companies the opportunity of obtaining High Court protection from their creditors for a limited period of time while the prospects of putting together a survival package are investigated by an independent, court-appointed examiner. In some respects the Act is similar to the court administration process available in the UK under the Insolvency Act 1986 and the procedures provided for in Chapter 11 of the US Bankruptcy Act 1987.

Companies may encounter a variety of difficulties, which may lead to collapse. Bad management, mismatched funding, insufficient cash or profit margins, or involvement in 'disaster projects' are commercial mistakes which are corrected more by education and experience than by legislation. Often the use of the 1990 Act in attempts to resolve such inherent difficulties is inappropriate or too late. The fact that a number of examinerships have been unsuccessful is as much due to the unsuitability of the companies involved as 'patients' as to other factors. The legislation, described by some as a statutory bypass for ailing companies (but with the examiner acting as consultant physician rather than surgeon), cannot cure companies who wait until they are financially at death's door; nor can it be expected to help companies riddled with other illnesses. It is thus somewhat unfair to suggest that the legislation has failed; it is the approach taken by companies which is often inappropriate.

The Act provides a relatively quick and streamlined method of helping companies worthy of assistance who have been unfortunate rather than inept. As such it is to be welcomed. That the philosophy behind the Act requires the freezing of debts and the alteration of traditional priorities is a matter of considerable concern here (particularly to secured creditors). It is unreal to expect a radical change of attitude in the business community to occur overnight. Furthermore, it has been suggested that the interference with the rights of creditors may be constitutionally unsound, although arguments based on the common good of all the creditors (and the company's employees) are also sustainable. The Act, therefore, is not without its problems or its critics. Perhaps improvements could be made; for example, by allowing examiners a more direct involvement in the management of the company during the protection period, or by tightening up the process by which expenses can be certified. But in essence the Act is capable of being used effectively in appropriate circumstances for the right reasons: to rescue deserving companies. Above all, the examinership procedure is subject to the supervision of the court, which should ensure its operation in a fair and equitable manner.

Several people have helped me with this work. I hope it is not invidious to mention Bill Shipsey and Barry O'Neill as being especially helpful and encouraging. I am grateful also to many other colleagues at the Law Library and members of the solicitors' profession. Paddy McSwiney and John Donnelly were also of considerable assistance. The staff of the Law Library were unfailingly courteous and helpful. Thanks also to Mary Mulvany for her careful preparation of the manuscript and to Gerard O'Connor of Oak Tree Press for his patience and forbearance. Finally, I am grateful to the Chief Justice, the Honourable Mr Justice Thomas A. Finlay, for his graceful foreword, and most of all to my family, without whom this book would simply not have been possible.

St Brigid's Day, 1994

Table of Cases

Table of Statutes

Note: References in bold indicate where the text of an Act or a statutory provision is set out

1. ACTS OF THE OIREACHTAS

2. ACTS OF THE UNITED KINGDOM PARLIAMENT

3. RULES OF THE SUPERIOR COURTS

CHAPTER 1

The Presentation of the Petition

The period of protection available to a company under the Act commences not by order of the court but by the presentation of the petition in the Central Office.[1] The period of protection runs for three months from that date[2] unless or until the petition is withdrawn, or refused by the court. In view of the wide-ranging effect that such protection has on creditors and others associated with the company, the obtaining of protection by such a relatively simple administrative process without any immediate court sanction may to some extent appear unsatisfactory. The rules of the Superior Courts[3] now provide a procedure which regulates the presentation of the petition and the steps to be taken thereafter.

Types of Companies in Respect of which a Petition may be Presented

Since the Act is to be construed in conjunction with the other Companies Acts as one Act, it appears that any company formed and registered in Ireland under the 1963 Act (or any company formed under pre-existing legislation[4] which is still in existence) is entitled to be granted protection under the Act.[5] No definition of 'company' is contained in the Act except that a 'related company' is defined in the section giving power to the court to appoint an examiner to such a company as including any body which may be wound up by the High Court.[6] Thus, a company registered abroad (even if it has a place of business here) would not appear to be covered.

Certain companies incorporated under other legislation may be granted protection (e.g. a banking company holding a banking licence under section 9 of the Central Bank Act 1971) but the petition may only be presented by a particular party (e.g. the Central Bank).[7]

1. Section 5 (1) of the Companies (Amendment) Act 1990 (hereinafter referred to as 'the Act').
2. Unless extended under section 18.
3. Order 75A (SI No. 147 of 1991) hereinafter referred to as 'the rules'.
4. Such as the Companies (Consolidation) Act 1908, the Companies Act 1862 and the Joint Stock Companies Acts 1856-57.
5. Section 2.   6. Section 6(6).
7. Section 3(2)(a) and (b).

The court may enforce a reorganisation or reconstruction order made by a court in another country (recognised by Ministerial Order) in respect of a company incorporated in that country. In this way Irish courts can give effect to similar procedures taking place elsewhere which affect foreign-based companies with branches located in Ireland.[8]

Format and Contents of the Petition

While no specific form is provided for the petition, the rules indicate that it should as far as applicable comply with Form No. 2 of Appendix M of the 1986 rules.[9] The petition must thus state the full name and address of the petitioner, his capacity (e.g. creditor, contributory etc.) and list the date of incorporation, registered office, nominal and paid up share capital and objects of the company. In addition, there are a number of other requirements set out in the Act with which the petition must comply.

Firstly, the Act requires that it be shown to the court that the company is or is likely to be unable to pay its debts.[10] The company is deemed to be in this position[11] if (a) it is unable to pay its debts as they fall due, (b) the value of its assets is less than the amount of its liabilities (including contingent and prospective liabilities), or (c) if (under section 214 of the Principal Act) a properly served demand for payment of in excess of £1,000 by a creditor remains unpaid or unsatisfied, or an attempt to execute or process a judgment against the company has been returned unsatisfied.[12] In considering whether or not the company is or is likely to be unable to pay its debts, the court may consider whether significant extensions of time have been sought by the company from its creditors to pay its debts. What will constitute a 'significant' extension is probably a matter of degree in every case, but an extension substantially beyond the time normally allowed in a particular business or between the relevant parties is likely to be 'significant' if not otherwise explained. The nature and extent of the demands for payment made by creditors will also be relevant, as will the extent of the company's indebtedness.

There is no 'and' inserted between section 2(3)(a) and section 2(3)(b);[13]

---

8.   Section 36.
9.   Rule 4(3).
10.   Section 2(1)(a).
11.   Section 2(3).
12.   Non-payment of a debt because the debt is *bona fide* disputed is not neglect under the section — *Re Lympne Investments Ltd* [1972] 1WLR 523.
13.   *Re Creation Printing Limited* (1981) IR 353.

such an insertion might present considerable difficulties to a petitioner, since the value of the company's assets need not necessarily be lower than its liabilities to render it unable to pay its debts. A company's assets in 'book-value' terms may exceed the value of its liabilities; yet because of cash-flow difficulties, problems in an associated company, a down-turn in trade or other reasons the company may be unable to pay its debts *as they fall due*, perhaps because its assets cannot be readily realised, or if realised would have to be sold at an under-value.[14] This inability to pay debts as *they fall due* means that the company is technically insolvent.

Evidence of an unsatisfied demand or unsatisfied execution of a judgment under section 214 is compelling evidence of a company's inability to pay its debts.

Thus, in addition to the formal matters set out above, the petition should refer to:

> (i) the company's inability to pay its debts as they fall due, including whether or not negotiations or extensions have been requested or granted by creditors,
> (ii) the statement of the company's assets and liabilities, and their relative value at present,
> (iii) (where relevant) whether section 214(a) or (b) applies to the company.

The petition should also indicate (iv) whether or not a resolution for the winding up of the company subsists,[15] and (v) whether any order winding up the company has been made,[16] since both these matters should be negatived before the court has power to appoint an examiner.

However, the court is also particularly empowered to make an order appointing an examiner if it is shown that such an order would be likely to facilitate the survival of the company (and the whole or any part of its undertaking) as a going concern.[17] As will be seen later, the onus of proof on the petitioner is less exacting in this regard than in the UK. It is suggested that some attempt should be made in the petition to explain how the making of an order would facilitate the survival of the company as set out above. Evidence of the continued growth of the company's business, interest from potential investors, favourable reaction from financiers and/or creditors, a predicted improvement in market conditions as well as other factors may

14. *Re European Life Assurance Society* (1869) LR 9 Eq 122.
15. Section 2(1)(b).
16. Section 2(1)(c).
17. Section 2(2).

all be relevant in attempting to show that a company (and the whole or part of its undertaking) is capable of survival as a going concern provided it is given the time and protection afforded by a court order under the Act. A petitioning creditor may, of course, know little about the future prospects of a company. He will be unlikely to be able to say whether or not the order might facilitate the survival of the company. However, since the only positive requirement which the petitioner must fulfil is to show the court that the company is or is unlikely to be able to pay its debts,[18] his lack of knowledge about the company's future is not necessarily fatal.

But a petition must show (or be supported by) evidence that the petitioner has 'good reason' to require the appointment of an examiner.[19] In the absence of (or in addition to) expressing a particular view as to the specific future prospects of the company in any detail, it is submitted that a petitioner may fulfil this requirement in other ways. He may point to the actual or imminent appointment of a receiver over the assets of the company, to threats of liquidation, or to litigation which has commenced against the company which he can establish should probably be stayed pending the appointment of an examiner. He may also be able to show that a judgment creditor in the process of executing his judgment against the company will remove all the available assets from the company. What will constitute 'good reason' will depend on the facts and circumstances of each individual case as the court may see fit.

The petition should also nominate a person to be appointed as examiner, who has consented to act.[20]

As we will see, a number of different parties are given the power to present a petition. In the case of a petition presented by the company or the directors of the company, the petition must include a statement of assets and liabilities of the company in so far as they are known to the petitioner(s) as they stand on a date not earlier than seven days before the presentation of the petition. In this, as in every other matter referred to in the petition, the petitioner(s) is obliged to exercise the utmost good faith and to disclose all relevant facts material to the exercise of the court's discretion.[21] Since the petition is presented to the court initially on an *ex parte* basis, the court relies to a considerable extent on the truth of its contents. Accidental errors

---

18.   See in particular the judgment of McCarthy J. in *Re Atlantic Magnetics Ltd*, Supreme Court (unreported) 5 December 1991.
19.   Section 3(3).
20.   Section 3(3)(a).
21.   See *Re Selukwe Ltd*, High Court (unreported), 20 December 1991 (Costello J.); *Re Wogans (Drogheda) Ltd (No. 2)*, High Court (unreported) 7 May 1992 (Costello J.).

or omissions may not be fatal, but deliberate omissions or breaches of this duty to exercise good faith are likely to be held to amount to an abuse of the process of the court. While a simple statement of the total value of the assets and the total value of the liabilities may be set out in the petition, the affidavit verifying the petition should set out in more detail how these values are arrived at; perhaps a modification of the format used for a statement of affairs is more appropriate. It is desirable that, whether the petition is brought by the company, its directors or any other qualified person, as much relevant information as possible should be contained in the petition and verifying affidavit. The circumstances and background to the company's present difficulties are almost always relevant to some degree or other, as are its dealings with creditors and its financial (or even, on occasions, internal) difficulties. In addition, any attempts to resolve the company's problems by way of a proposed scheme or arrangement or otherwise should also be referred to.

The Verifying Affidavit

Again, no format is specified for this although it is clear from the rules that the petition must be verified by affidavit.[22] But whereas the form provided for an affidavit verifying a winding-up petition is extremely short, it is submitted that considerably more detail will be required in an affidavit verifying a petition to appoint an examiner.

The affidavit should be sworn by the petitioner, or petitioners if more than one, or if presented by a company, by a director, secretary or other officer. When a petition is presented by the directors of the company (or a majority thereof), one of their number can swear the verifying affidavit; presumably the position in respect of shareholders is the same.[23]

Ideally, the affidavit should amplify in more detail the various matters referred to in the petition. The affidavit can exhibit such items as correspondence with creditors, letters of demand and deeds of mortgage and charge under which a receiver is (or is about to be) appointed, as well as other relevant material. The resolution of the members or of the board of directors to present a petition can also be exhibited. Bearing in mind yet again the *uberrima fides* nature of the application, the affidavit should also contain as much detailed relevant information as practicable.

A contingent or prospective creditor may require additional evidence to

---

22.   Rule 4(3).
23.   See *Re Don Bluth Entertainment Ltd (No. 1)*, High Court (unreported) 27 August 1992 (Murphy J.); see also *Re Equiticorp International plc* [1989] BCLC 597.

satisfy a court as to security for the costs of the petition as well as to make out a *prima facie* case for court protection.[24] There are no Irish cases on what constitutes a *prima facie* case in this context; the identification and establishment of a 'reasonable prospect' of survival for the company will almost certainly suffice.

It may be the case that a company in difficulty has already had meetings with creditors, and has begun to negotiate possible terms under which its difficulties could be resolved. These discussions may be continuing at the time of the presentation of the petition. But it will often be prudent for a company to have obtained financial advice from an independent adviser in the course of its difficulties, and if this has resulted in the preparation of a set of proposals for a compromise or scheme of arrangement to be submitted to interested parties, a copy of these proposals must be exhibited to the affidavit.[25] Otherwise, business plans and projections may also be of assistance. Attempts by a company to obtain financial advice and to act on this advice during troublesome times will often be evidence of a responsible and *bona fide* approach.

The affidavit should also exhibit the consent of the person nominated as examiner to act;[26] it is appropriate to have an affidavit of fitness prepared also. In addition, the affidavit should show how the appointment of an examiner will facilitate the survival of the company and will be in the interests of its creditors and members. It may be necessary to deal specifically with the perceived advantages of the appointment of an examiner where a receiver is (or is about to be) appointed.[27]

The affidavit must be sworn before the petition is presented, though additional affidavits may also be subsequently filed.

While the Act does not specifically envisage the appointment of a 'provisional examiner', the rules do provide for the appointment of an examiner on an interim basis pending the hearing of the petition. If such an interim appointment is sought, the reasons for this will be required to be set out in detail in the verifying affidavit (or, if desired, in a separate affidavit). This type of application will be dealt with later.

---

24.   Section 3(5).
25.   Section 3(4)(b).
26.   Section 3(4)(a).
27   As the receiver's principal concern is to realise funds in order to pay the debenture-holder, a petitioner may be apprehensive that the company will cease to trade while the assets are being sold. Difficulties may also be encounterd in collecting from debtors and the very fact that the company is in receivership may itself cause other associated difficulties for the company.

Who May Present the Petition

The following parties may present a petition seeking court protection:

(a) The company.[28]

A resolution of the majority of the members is probably required.

(b) The directors of the company.[29]

It has been well established that the directors of a company do not have the power to present a petition to wind up a company unless their decision has been ratified by the members.[30] The Act now specifically empowers the directors of the company seeking protection to present a petition. It is not necessary that all of the directors shall have voted unanimously in favour of the decision to present a petition or that they must all present the petition together. In *Re Don Bluth Entertainment Ltd (No. 1)*[31] it was held that once there had been a valid resolution passed by a properly convened meeting of the board of directors to present a petition, any one or all of the directors could exercise that function.

(c) Creditors of the company.[32]

A creditor may need to establish that a debt is owed to it, since earlier authorities suggest that a creditor's petition may be dismissed if its claim has been disputed in good faith and on substantial grounds by the company.[33]

While a contingent or prospective creditor[34] (including an employee) may also present a petition under this section, he will be required to establish a *prima facie* case for court protection and may be obliged to give such security for costs as the court thinks is reasonable.

(d) Members of the company.[35]

Oppression of a member does not of itself confer a right on a member to

28. Section 3(1)(a).
29. Section 3(1)(b).
30. See *Re Galway Tramhill Co.* (1918) 52 ILTR 41 and *Re Cannock Ltd*, High Court (unreported) 8th September, 1984 (Murphy J.). The principle was adopted in England in *Re Emmadart Ltd* [1979] 1 All ER 599.
31. High Court (unreported) 27 August 1992 (Murphy J.). See also *Re Equiticorp International plc* [1989] BCLC 597.
32. Section 3(1)(c).
33. *Re Pageboy Couriers Ltd* [1983] ILRM 510.
34. For what constitutes a contingent or prospective creditor see *Stonegate Securities v Gregory* [1980] 1 All ER 241.
35. Section 3(1)(d).

present a petition seeking court protection. Under the Act, in order to present a petition a member (or members) must hold not less than one-tenth of the paid up capital of the company carrying the right of voting at general meetings as of the date of the presentation of such a petition.

All or any of the above parties may present a petition together or separately. However, the reference to 'all or any' probably does not have sufficient strength to mean that some or even one director could present a petition without a proper board resolution having first been passed.[36]

Two other parties who are entitled to seek court protection for certain types of companies deserve mention. Where the company requiring protection is an insurer, only the Minister for Enterprise and Employment is permitted to present the petition. Similarly, where the company in question holds a Banking Licence under section 9 of The Central Bank Act 1971, or is otherwise under the supervision of the Central Bank by any other enactment (e.g. an industrial and provident society), the petition may only be presented by the Central Bank.[37]

The petition and affidavit should be presented and filed at the Central Office. It will there be assigned by the relevant registrar to a particular judge.[38]

Notice of the petition should also be delivered by the petitioner to the Registrar of Companies within three days of presentation.[39]

Application for Directions

As already indicated, the period of protection commences with the presentation of the petition. While many companies may require the appointment of an examiner on an interim basis even prior to the hearing of the petition, there will undoubtedly be companies for whom the presentation of the petition in the Central Office alone will provide a panacea (however short term) for their ills. However, the petitioner is now obliged on the same day as the petition is presented to apply to the court for directions.

This application is *ex parte*, and again the duty to disclose all relevant information to the court exists. Primarily the purpose is to obtain directions from the court as to how the existence of the petition should be notified. The winding-up rules[40] set out detailed provisions as to the time and mode

36.   See *Re Equiticorp International plc* above. See also *Re Instrumentation Electrical Services Ltd* [1988] BCLC 550.
37.   Section 3(2).
38.   Rule 4. See also Practice Direction, 5 September 1992.
39.   See section 12(1).
40.   See order 74, rules 10 and 11 of the rules of the Superior Courts.

of service, and these will normally be followed in a modified fashion. For example, the court will usually direct that the petition be advertised in two national daily newspapers. The hearing of the petition is usually fixed for a Monday, but the court may also order that particular parties be served with copies of the petition and affidavit. So, where a receiver stands appointed already, he will normally be a notice-party (as will the creditor who appointed him). If the petition is presented by a party other than the company, the court will direct that the company be served. A dispute between the company (or its directors or shareholders) and a particular creditor may have given rise to the company's current insolvent position. In such a situation, the relevant creditor is also likely to be made a notice-party. The court may direct that other parties also be served, depending on the circumstances of the particular case; the matter is within the discretion of the court.

In fixing the time and mode of service (and advertisement) the court will balance the need for the giving of adequate notice to the parties concerned against the fact that the presentation of the petition already prevents creditors from exercising their normal rights with the consequent risk of injustice.[41] As a result, the court will usually be anxious that service is effected as expeditiously as possible, and the date for hearing will be fixed according to similar considerations.

Hearings *In Camera*

Since the court has power to direct that the petition should not, in the interests of justice, be heard in public, it is possible that advertisements will not be directed, or other restrictions may be imposed.[42] In so directing, however, the court must consider that the interests of the company concerned or its creditors as a whole require this. The power applies not just to the hearing of the petition but also to the whole or part of any proceedings under the Act. The discretion to make such an order is even less likely to be exercised since *Re R. Ltd*,[43] where it was held that a party seeking to have a matter heard *in camera* must show not only that the disclosure of information would be seriously prejudicial to the company (or its creditors) but also that a public hearing of the proceedings which it seeks to have heard

41.   See *Re Rowbotham Baxter* (1990) BCLC 397.
42.   Section 31. In *Re Goodman International Ltd*, High Court (unreported) 29 August 1990, the petition was presented and an examiner appointed at a sitting of the High Court (Hamilton P.) in the judge's home
43.   (1989) IR 126.

in camera would fall short of the proper administration of justice.[44] It may even be inappropriate to decide the issue of whether or not the proceedings should be heard *in camera* on an *ex parte* application.

In addition to obtaining directions, the opportunity of this *ex parte* application is often used by the petitioner to apply for the appointment of an examiner on an interim basis. This is now considered in more detail.

Appointment of Interim Examiner

While the Act did not expressly provide for the appointment of an examiner on an interim basis, the rules have now provided a method by which such an appointment can be made at the hearing of the application for directions.[45] A court may, of course, treat the application as the hearing of the petition and make any order it sees fit (including, presumably, an order appointing the examiner on a 'full' basis) but this is rarely done, and any appointment at this stage is likely to be for an interim period only.

Even on an interim basis, however, an examiner so appointed would appear to have all the powers conferred by the Act on the examiner.[46] His primary function must be to examine the affairs of the company; he does not take over any of the management functions or powers unless expressly authorised to do so by the court. But he is given certain specific powers in the Act which he appears to be entitled to exercise even on an interim basis. Perhaps the most controversial of these, at this stage, is his power to certify liabilities incurred by the company as having been necessarily and properly incurred.[47]

The effect of the exercise of this power will be considered in more detail below. In summary, it means that an expense incurred by a company which is certified at the time it is incurred by the examiner will be paid in full (unless a court orders otherwise) ahead of any other claim made against the company. An examiner is thus in a position to accord a priority over all other debts including secured and preferential debts[48] to an expense incurred by certifying it under section 10. Given that such a sweeping power is immediately available to him, a court may be reluctant to appoint an examiner (even on an interim basis) without a full hearing of the petition.

44. At page 137 (Walsh J). The application was made in that case under section 205(7) of the 1963 Act.
45. Rule 5(2). A court was empowered to appoint a provisional liquidator under section 226(1) of the 1963 Act. See also Order 74, rule 14 of the rules of the Superior Court.
46. A court can limit and restrict the powers of a provisional liquidator — see section 226(2).
47. Section 10.
48. Except his own remuneration and costs — see section 29.

For some companies the protection invoked by the presentation of the petition may be sufficient. For other companies the admission of its insolvency and inability to pay debts due may present very significant problems. Firstly, such a company may have insufficient monies available to meet day-to-day expenses, especially if its insolvency is particularly serious. It may have difficulties in obtaining payments from debtors and it is unlikely to have further monies advanced to it from lending institutions or other financial sources. Yet meeting day-to-day expenses (e.g. electricity, telephone or transport costs) or obtaining additional funding (e.g. for wages or associated production costs) may be crucial to the company's survival even in the short term. Only an examiner can certify that the expenses in question are properly incurred, and he can only do so at the time they are incurred; if the expenses are to be incurred in the interim period, they cannot afterwards be sanctioned by an examiner appointed after a full hearing of the petition. So if interim expenses are to be incurred and certified, an interim examiner must be appointed.

The court will thus balance the effect of the power of certification against the need of the company to incur such expenses in the interim period. But where the company's survival as a going concern even during the interim period would be severely prejudiced by its inability to incur expenses or obtain funding, it is submitted that a court would be slow to refuse to appoint an interim examiner. As the discretion given to the court is extremely wide,[49] it is submitted that the court could limit the powers of an interim examiner by (for example) limiting the amount or nature of the expenses which he could certify as being properly incurred expenses until the hearing of the petition, or by other terms as it sees fit.[50]

Thus, it is suggested that if a petitioner wishes to have an interim examiner appointed, the verifying affidavit should deal specifically with this matter. It may thus be necessary to show (i) the lack of alternative available funding, (ii) the need to incur expenses or obtain funding during the interim period to ensure the company's survival, (iii) the extent (if known) to which creditors or persons dealing with the company are prepared to continue so dealing while the company is under court protection, (iv) an estimate of the amount of expenses it is thought it will be necessary to incur prior to the hearing of the petition, and (v) whether other ancillary orders are required.[51]

The examiner's duties (as well as his powers) also take effect from the

49.   Rule 5(2).
50.   Section 29 also appears to allow the court to impose such a limitation.
51.   E.g. a direction that a receiver who already stands appointed should cease to act further.

date of his appointment even though the appointment is on an interim basis only. Thus, his obligation to prepare the report for the court within 21 days and to formulate proposals, put them before meetings and report back to the court again within 42 days[52] runs from the date of his appointment, not the date of the presentation or hearing of the petition.

An interim examiner may find that, contrary to earlier indications, the company is incapable of survival as a going concern, or that materially misleading or false information was given to the court on the earlier application. This should be brought to the attention of the court immediately, if necessary by re-entering the application or applying himself. An interim examiner is an officer of the court with the same duties of impartiality and honesty; no professional qualifications are required and the only disqualificatory matters are those which would also prevent a person acting as liquidator.[53]

While technically an interim examiner should advertise his appointment also,[54] in practice this can be included in the advertisement which advertises the petition, the principle behind the section being the importance of notification that the company is under court protection and has had an examiner appointed. If his appointment is confirmed at the hearing of the petition, he may advertise this subsequently.

Once appointed, the interim examiner may start examining the company's affairs with a view to seeing how the survival of the company as a going concern may be achieved. The time period which elapses between his appointment and the hearing of the petition may be short, but even within that time he may make progress in negotiation with creditors and potential investors. It is therefore appropriate for an interim examiner to prepare an interim report stating whether or not he thinks the company is capable of survival which he can present to the court at the hearing of the petition, since a court in making what is essentially a commercial decision must necessarily place considerable reliance on the views of an insolvency practitioner in such a situation.[55] Indeed, even if no interim examiner is appointed, a report prepared by an independent expert may be helpful in this regard.

52.   Section 15 and section 18 respectively. These time limits can be extended by the court.
53.   Section 28.
54.   Section 12(2).
55.   *Re Primlaks (UK) Ltd* [1989] BCLC 734.

CHAPTER 2

The Hearing of the Petition

While the court has a discretion to treat the application for directions as the hearing of the petition, this discretion will rarely be exercised. The purpose of the petition is to give parties an opportunity to be heard. The appointment of an examiner has such a wide-ranging effect that to make such an order on the basis of an *ex parte* application would be extremely unusual. As already pointed out, the need for certification of expenses pending the hearing of the petition can be met by the appointment of an interim examiner.

In a manner similar to that set out in the UK Act of 1986, the Act gives the examination process priority over other processes. Since no proceedings for the winding-up of the company can be commenced once a petition seeking protection has been presented,[1] it will not be possible to present or hear a winding-up petition until the petition seeking protection has been dealt with. Even a winding-up petition which was presented *before* a petition seeking protection does not receive priority; the Act says that both petitions shall be heard together.[2] It is contrary to the whole essence of the examination process that anything be done pending the hearing of a petition seeking protection which might damage (or might be seen in public to damage) the company. An attempt to advertise a winding-up petition was restrained on this basis in England.[3]

There are a couple of situations in which a court may refuse to hear a petition. For example, a contingent or prospective creditor's petition may not be heard if the creditor has not given reasonable security for costs as fixed by the court or has not established a *prima facie* case for protection.[4] Nor can a court hear a petition if prior to the presentation of the petition a receiver stands and has stood appointed to the company for a continuous period of at least three days.[5] The period was initially 14 days but was

---

1.   Section 5(2)(1).   2. Section 6(5).
3.   In *Re A company* [1989] BCLC 9. A company giving an undertaking to present a petition seeking protection might also prevent a winding-up petition being advertised — *Re A company* [1989] BCLC 715.
4.   Section 3(5).   5. Section 3(6).

reduced by section 180(1)(a) of the Companies Act 1990. The aim of shortening the period in question was to provide a greater degree of certainty for receivers, though the effect is probably to galvanise petitioners into action more quickly. Debenture-holders may seek to appoint more receivers on Thursdays or Fridays, but this tactic can be countered by presenting a petition to a High Court judge at a special sitting on a Saturday or Sunday.[6] It is also clear that the High Court may decide to remit a petition to the Circuit Court if it appears that the total liabilities of the company do not exceed £250,000.[7] This discretion can be excerised by the High Court at any stage in the course of the proceedings. It appears to be an attempt to reduce costs and to decentralise matters from the High Court in Dublin, though it has never as yet been used.

Neither the Act nor the rules specify the parties who are entitled or obliged to appear on the hearing of the petition. The rules allow the court to adjourn the hearing until any party or parties which the court feels should be notified of the petition have been notified.[8] Indeed, the court has power to adjourn the hearing of the petition for any reason which appears to it to be just and equitable. There does not appear to be a requirement to give notice of intention to appear. All members and creditors of a company will almost certainly be entitled to appear and to be heard as of right, and contingent or prospective creditors may also be heard as the court sees fit. It is likely that a receiver or provisional liquidator will also be heard since the court may have to make orders specifically dealing with their positions if an examiner is ultimately appointed.[9] One of the significant distinguishing features of the Irish legislation is that no veto is given to any particular creditor or member, or indeed to any other party. Section 9(3) of the UK Insolvency Act 1986 compels a court to dismiss a petition where an administrative receiver has been appointed, unless the appointor consents to the making of an administration order or there is some fatal defect in the security appointing the receiver. In *Re A company (No. 00175 of 1987)*[10] time was given to a secured creditor to decide whether or not to appoint an administrative receiver before this power was extinguished, since Vinclott J. held that the legislature must have intended that a secured creditor be given an adequate opportunity to consider this option. No such

6.   As occurred in *Atlantic Magnetics*.
7.   Section 3(9). The appropriate circuit is the circuit where the company has its registered office or principal place of business.
8.   Rule 5(3).
9.   Section 6.
10.   [1987] BCLC 467. The decision (based on section 9(2) of that Act) highlights some of the differences between the UK and Irish legislation.

preferential treatment is given to any party under the Irish legislation; the legislature clearly did not intend that the fate of the company and those who depend on it should lie in the hands of one (or more) secured creditors.[11] While it is unlikely that a secured creditor would not be notified of the petition, he has no statutory veto. The same is true of creditors who would be preferential in a winding-up (e.g. the Revenue Commissioners, or employees of the company).

The court has extremely wide powers at the hearing of the petition under the legislation. It may, for example, adjourn the hearing (conditionally or unconditionally) or make any other interim order it thinks fit.[12] One can envisage a petition being adjourned if the court requires other parties to be notified, or if negotiations are taking place which might ultimately mean court protection was no longer necessary (because, for example, the requested funds had been made available). Adjournments of this nature will generally be short because of the extraordinary effect of court protection as well as the limited period for which it is available. Conditions which may be imposed may refer to the interim examiner's powers, the position of a receiver or provisional liquidator, or any other matter which the court sees fit. Generally, however, the issue for the court to decide is whether to dismiss the petition or to allow it and appoint an examiner.

Since the exercise of the court's discretion is of considerable importance, the decision of the Supreme Court in *Re Atlantic Magnetics Ltd*[13] is of significance. This was the first occasion on which the Supreme Court was asked to consider the extent to which a petitioner seeking court protection for a company must establish the prospects for survival of that company if protection is granted. A number of English decisions suggested that a 'real prospect' of survival (or one of the other objectives stated in section 8 of the UK Insolvency Act) must be established before an administration order will be made.[14] Some decisions suggested that the onus is even more burdensome, requiring that the evidence should show that the objective will 'more probably than not' be achieved.[15] Both of these tests were rejected by the Supreme Court. In the High Court Lardner J. had expressed the view that in some cases the evidence may make it clear that survival is not a practical possibility, while in others a strong possibility of

11.   See in particular the judgment of McCarthy J. in *Atlantic Magnetics*.
12.   Section 3(7).
13.   Supreme Court (unreported) 5 December 1991.
14.   See *Re Consumer and Industrial Press Ltd* [1988] BCLC 177. See also *Re Harris Simmons Construction Ltd* [1989] BCLC 202; *Re Primlaks (UK) Ltd* [1989] BCLC 735; and *Re SCL Building Services Ltd* [1990] BCLC 98.
15.   See *Re Consumer and Industrial Press* (above).

an adjustment which will allow the company to survive will be apparent. Where there is no clear-cut conclusion (or indeed a conflict on the evidence), he held that the standard to be applied was whether in all the circumstances it was worthwhile to order an investigation of the company's affairs by an examiner, there being some reasonable prospect of survival.

Finlay C.J.[16] qualified this test only by suggesting that 'some prospect' of survival be established. McCarthy J.[17] rejected the 'real prospect' test completely, suggesting that no firm conclusion could be reached on the company's prospects until an examiner had carried out his task of preliminary examination and had furnished his first statutory report to the courts. Both judgments referred to the short time frame allowed by the legislation for examination, as well as to the need to balance the rights of the different creditors, employees and the company itself.

The wide discretion conferred on the court by the Act as to how the power to appoint an examiner should be exercised is in sharp contrast to the UK legislation. The only guidance given to Irish courts appears in section 2(2) of the Act where the court is empowered particularly to appoint an examiner if it considers that such an appointment would be likely to facilitate the survival of the company (or any part of it) as a going concern. Finlay C.J. regarded this as a 'strongly persuasive obligation'[18] to make such an order where it was likely that the company's survival would so be facilitated. Section 8 of the UK Insolvency Act 1986, on the other hand, sets out the specific purposes for which (and only for which) an administration order[19] must be made, and the order so made must specify the particular purpose or purposes for which it was made.

As a result of this decision, it appears that a court should be slow to exercise its discretion against a petitioner seeking the appointment of an examiner unless the circumstances indicate that there is no identifiable possibility of survival. Arguably, of course, any company could claim that it *could* survive if the circumstances were favourable, and it is submitted that any prospect of survival identified should be practical rather than far-fetched.[20] It may also be that a number of unsuccessful efforts to save

16.   With whom Egan, and O'Flaherty J.J. agreed.
17.   With whom Egan J. also agreed.
18.   At page 7 of the judgment.
19.   The equivalent of the appointment of an examiner for these purposes.
20.   In *Re Rex Rotary (Ireland) Ltd* (Supreme Court (unreported) 19 May 1992 *ex tempore*) Finlay C.J. referred to an 'identifiable' prospect of survival. The court refused to appoint an examiner to a company, concluding that the proposals put forward for a possible scheme of arrangement were much too tentative. The appointment had been

the company have already been made prior to the presentation of the petition seeking protection. A court is also likely to give weight to the views of a receiver or a provisional liquidator who is already familiar with the company's affairs in coming to its decision. Similarly, any report compiled by an interim examiner will be of assistance to the court. In making what is essentially a commercial decision, the court must necessarily place considerable reliance on the views of an insolvency practitioner in such a situation.[21] The court will also consider the views of the various members and creditors. In England it has been held that a court can take into account the likelihood or otherwise of the necessary majorities being obtained at the statutory meeting of creditors to approve proposals for a scheme of arrangement.[22] The Act does not provide that any particular additional weight[23] be given to any class or category of creditors and it has been accepted that the interests of secured creditors may weigh lighter in the scales than the interests of other creditors when a court is asked to appoint an examiner.[24]

Ultimately, the exercise of the court's discretion will depend on the circumstances of the individual case, though the decision in *Atlantic Magnetics* indicates an examiner should probably be appointed unless there are strong reasons for doing otherwise.

Once it decides to accede to the petition and to appoint an examiner, the court is empowered to make a number of other orders to deal with the position of the provisional liquidator or receiver.[25] Ancillary orders relating to the powers of the examiner may also be required at this stage. In theory the court can make all or any of these orders at the application for directions stage, though in practice they are more usually made on the hearing of the petition.

Receiver

Since the principal concern of a receiver who stands appointed to a company

opposed by a secured creditor, a financial institution which had previously provided funding to the company. See *Sunday Business Post*, 24 May 1992.

21.   *Re Primlaks UK Ltd* (footnote 14, above) at page 747.
22.   *Re Land and Property Trust company (No. 2)* [1991] BCLC 849.
23.   See *Re Pye (Ireland) Ltd*, Supreme Court (unreported), 17 April 1985 (*ex tempore*) reversing High Court (unreported), 11 March 1985 (Costello J.). See also *Re Pye (Ireland) Ltd*, High Court (unreported), 12 November 1984 (Costello J.).
24.   *Re Consumer and Industrial Press Ltd* above and *Re Imperial Motors (UK) Ltd* [1990] BCLC 29. See also McCarthy J.'s judgement in *Atlantic Magnetics* (footnote 13 above).
25.   Section 3(1)(a).

or the whole or part of its undertaking or property) will be to realise funds for the debenture-holder,[25a] certain steps may have to be taken to prevent the receiver from doing anything which would prejudice the survival of the company as a going concern during the protection period. He may, for example, have ceased to trade or advertised assets for sale. A receiver may thus be directed to cease to act from a specified date. A less extreme form of restriction would be a direction that he act as receiver only in respect of certain specified assets.[26] Such a situation can be envisaged where a court is told that only part of the undertaking of a company can survive — a receiver might then be allowed to continue to act in respect of the remainder of the assets. A receiver may also be ordered to hand over to the examiner books and records relating to the company's property or undertaking, and to give particulars of any dealings he may have had in respect thereof.[27] The making of these orders (or such other order as the court sees fit) should clarify the position of the receiver as a result. The presentation of the petition effectively suspends any receivership unless (on the appointment of an examiner) the court gives the receiver specific powers under section 6. But the receivership may be reactivated if for any reason court protection is withdrawn.[28] In deciding whether to restrict the activities of a receiver, the court must have regard to whether such an order would be likely to facilitate the survival of the company (and the whole or part of its undertaking) as a going concern.[29] The Act does not expressly provide for the appointment of the receiver as examiner, perhaps because a conflict of interest might arise having regard to instructions previously received from the debenture-holder who appointed him.

Provisional Liquidator

While the Act provides for a prior winding-up petition to be heard together with the petition seeking protection where a provisional liquidator has *not* been appointed, there will be situations where a provisional liquidator has been appointed before the petition seeking protection is presented and heard. Again, clarification of his position is required if an examiner is appointed. Since a provisional liquidator is appointed by, and is an officer

---

25a.   See, in this regard, *Downsview Ltd v First City Corpn. Ltd* [1993] 2 WLR 86 and 97.

26.   Section 6(1)(b).   27.   Section 6(1)(c) and (d).

28.   In *Atlantic Magnetics* the examinership ceased and the receiver moved back in. In *United Meat Packers (and associated companies)*, Supreme Court (unreported), 13 March 1992 (*ex tempore*) the examiner also recommended the withdrawal of the court protection, and the receiver took over again.

29.   Section 6(3).

of, the court, a very real option available to the court at the hearing of the petition for protection is to appoint the provisional liquidator as examiner.[30] In addition to the necessary independence, a provisional liquidator will usually have the advantage of being familiar with the books and records and affairs generally of the company. This would be of particular relevance if no interim examiner had been appointed, since the appointment of a person already so acquainted with the company could result in a saving of fees and expenses. Alternatively, the court may (again having regard to whether such an order would be likely to facilitate the survival of the company or its undertaking as a going concern) direct the provisional liquidator to cease to act, and may also direct that he give all books and records as well as details of his dealings with the property or undertaking of the company to the examiner.[31]

Other ancillary orders relating to the effect of the appointment of an examiner on the position of a receiver or provisional liquidator may also be made by the court as it sees fit.[32]

Ancillary Orders Relating to Appointment of Examiner

The basic function of an examiner is to examine the situation, affairs and prospects of the company. Apart from the power to certify properly incurred expenses, an examiner has few other powers, but the court can (on the application of the examiner) vest certain other functions and powers in the examiner. The functions and powers of an examiner will be dealt with in chapter 4. For the present, it is sufficient to state that certain ancillary orders may be required at the hearing of the petition relating to the examiner. For example, it may be necessary or desirable that the court allow him to take over all or any of the functions and powers of the directors under section 9 or to dispose immediately of certain company assets under section 11. Specifically, an examiner may require power to borrow monies and may also seek a declaration that any such monies borrowed by him (or by the company) are to be treated as properly incurred expenses and so given priority under section 29. The Supreme Court approved the making of such a declaration in favour of an examiner in *Atlantic Magnetics*.[33] Since most of these (and other) additional powers and functions can only be granted by the court on the examiner's application, they are only likely to be dealt with at the petition stage if an interim examiner who has already been appointed so applies.

30.   Section 6(2)(a).   31.   Section 6(2)(c), (d) and (e).
32.   Section 6(4).
33.   At pages 14 and 19 of the judgment of Finlay C.J. referred to above.

Just as the court may confer additional powers and functions on the examiner, it may also restrict the exercise of his powers by imposing certain conditions. As the most controversial power is his power to certify expenses under section 10, the court may place an upper limit on the amount of money he should certify, or may direct that sanction under section 29 will only be granted to certified borrowings from a particular bank or source (e.g. a pre-existing secured creditor of the company) until further order.[34]

The court has a wide discretion under section 3(7) to make any other orders it sees fit. These could include the appointment of a committee of creditors,[35] or other directions relating to directors, creditors, members or the conduct of the business of the company generally.

Related Companies

It may be appropriate that an examiner be appointed not just to one company but to a whole group of companies because of the relationship between those companies. The business and trading history may make an entire group of companies interdependent for their continued existence on each other; or the economic and commercial realities may indicate that the companies have in fact carried on business as a single entity.[36] Section 4 of the Act allows an examiner to be appointed not just to an individual company but also to any related companies as the court sees fit. In making such an order the court must have regard to whether this would facilitate the survival of the company or the related company (or both) and the whole or any part of its or their undertaking as a going concern.[37]

This does not mean that the corporate veil between the related companies is automatically lifted. It is essentially a procedure to prevent a multiplicity of petitions, hearings and appointments for a group of companies where protection is required. It may be that some of the companies in a group can be salvaged while others cannot. The appointment of one examiner to the group of related companies is convenient from an administrative point of view as well as, hopefully, being cost-effective.

'Related' is defined in section 4(5). A company is deemed to be related to another company if the other company is its holding or subsidiary company, or where more than half of its equity share capital is held by the

---

34.   This was done in *Re Don Bluth Entertainment Ltd (No. 1)*, High Court (unreported), 27 August 1992 (Murphy J.).

35.   Section 21.

36.   See *Power Supermarkets Ltd v Crumlin Investments Ltd and Another*, High Court (unreported), 22 June 1981 (Costello J.).

37.   Section 4(2).

other company (and other related companies) or by members of the other company, or where more than half of the voting power at any of its general meetings can be exercised by that other company (and other related companies), or where it is not possible to identify readily the separate business (or a substantial part thereof) of each company because of the manner in which the businesses of the companies have been carried on, or where there is another body corporate to which both companies are related. The phrase 'body corporate' was deliberately used to allow protection orders to be made where two Irish companies might be related to another body corporate (e.g. a foreign entity registered abroad).[38]

It is noteworthy that even if a protection order is made in respect of a related company the period of protection runs only from the date of the making of that order, rather than from the date of presentation of the petition in respect of the original company.[39] A related company may thus be somewhat exposed between the presentation of the original petition and the making of any order, but there is provision for the appointment of an interim examiner to a related company, and the court may make other directions as it sees fit.[40]

While the matter of costs is within the discretion of the court, a successful petitioner (other than the company) will usually be allowed its costs of the petition as against the company. This may be of little use if the company does not survive since there is no hierarchy determining what priority such costs should be given, unlike the rules relating to the winding-up of a company which set out the priority in which various costs should be paid.[41] Other parties who have been awarded costs for their attendance at the hearing of the petition are in a similar position. The examiner's costs are expressly provided for and given priority under section 29, and are usually the subject of a separate application. *See Chap. 5.*

Dismissal of the Petition

If the court decides not to appoint an examiner and to dismiss the petition, the immediate consequence is that the protection of the court is lifted from the company. Creditors are thus free again to pursue their own remedies.

So a receiver or a provisional liquidator may be appointed (or may return) to the company. Lifting protection does not automatically mean that

---

38.   The phrase was introduced by section 181(1)(b) of the Companies Act 1990.
39.   Section 4(3).
40.   Rule 6.
41.   Order 74, rule 128.

the company must be wound up, though if the petition for protection and a winding-up petition have been heard together under section 6(5) this may well be what will happen. Any interim examiner appointed appears to be automatically discharged by the dismissal of the petition, though he may be obliged to prepare a report on the company along the lines set out in section 16.[42] Since most interim examiners will probably already have presented a report to the court at the hearing of the petition, it seems unlikely that the court will require a further report after his appointment is discharged (except possibly for any application for costs and expenses under section 29).

In dismissing a petition, the court may award costs against the successful petitioner. Again, this is a matter within the discretion of the court. Directors acting in good faith who, doing their best to save the company, present a petition which is unsuccessful and subsequently appears ill-advised will not normally be penalised by an order to pay costs personally. But there may be exceptional circumstances where directors have acted so irresponsibly and in such flagrant breach of their duties as directors that such an order may be justified.[43] It is unlikely that an unsuccessful petitioner's costs would be ordered to be given any kind of priority in the costs of winding-up the company, though there may be special circumstances where this could occur.[44]

---

42.   Rule 7.
43.   *Re Land and Property Trust Co (No. 3)* [1991] BCLC 856.
44.   See *Re Merrytime (Ireland) Ltd*, High Court (unreported), (*ex tempore*), 29 June 1992 (Murphy J.), where the suggestion that the priority ranking of creditors was already destroyed by the superior ranking given to the examiner's remuneration, costs and expenses was rejected. Cf. *Re Gosscot (Ground works) Ltd* [1988] BCLC 363.

CHAPTER 3

The Effect of Court Protection

The principal effect of the presentation of the petition is to protect the company from its creditors. Protection is limited to the three month period set out in section 5 (subject to the specific extensions provided for in section 18) and may be ended sooner if the petition is subsequently withdrawn or refused. The company is thus provided with a breathing space to enable it to formulate a blueprint for survival in consultation with its members and creditors, while continuing to trade.

The Management and Running of the Company

Neither the presentation of the petition nor the appointment of an examiner have any direct effect on the management or running of the company. Unlike section 8(2) of the Insolvency Act 1986 in the UK, the examiner is not appointed to manage the affairs, business and property of the company, but only to examine the prospects for the company's survival: he is an officer of the court but not an officer of the company.[1] This may be a cause of considerable concern to creditors. If the company's insolvent position is due at least in part (as it usually is) to bad management, is it right that the same management team should be allowed to continue in control, possibly making matters worse? While this criticism is understandable, it is wrong to suggest that an examiner must of necessity always remains powerless to intervene in the management of the company. Section 9 expressly provides for the giving by the court to the examiner of all or any of the powers exercisable by the directors. In giving these powers to the examiner (and they can be given exclusively to him),[2] the court has a wide discretion; it may consider that the current conduct of the company's affairs may prejudice the interests of the company, its employees or creditors, or that such an order is necessary to preserve the assets and safeguard the interests of the company, or indeed may make the order on the basis of any other matter which appears relevant.[3] There is no requirement that the company

1. *Re Home Treats Ltd* [1990] BCLC 705.
2. Section 9(1).
3. Section 9(2). See also section 3(8).

or its directors have resolved that such an order should be sought, but this is a matter the court can also consider. The examiner can also be given the powers that a liquidator would have if he had been appointed as such in a winding-up by the court. There is thus considerable scope for expanding the powers of the examiner to include directorial powers where it is just and equitable to do so.

One reason why section 9 has been utilised so infrequently to date is the lack of information readily available to the examiner immediately after his appointment on how the company has been managed. Adding a direct managerial role to the examiner's functions is also likely to increase the cost of the examinership. However, it is submitted that examiners should not be slow to avail of this facility where necessary, particularly where there is evidence of gross incompetence on the part of the old management.[4]

The examiner may also exert an indirect influence on the management by his power to convene and preside at board meetings.[5]

Shareholders

Again, the position of the company's shareholders remains unaffected by court protection. Members can hold general meetings (which can be convened and attended by the examiner), transfer their shareholdings and exercise most other powers as shareholders during the protection period. They cannot, however, obtain any orders for relief (either against oppression or otherwise) under section 205,[6] either in respect of conduct before or during the protection period.

Employees

The commencement of court protection does not operate as a notice of discharge to the employees of a company.[7] It is submitted that service continues unbroken for the purposes of their statutory entitlements unless the company (or possibly, where so empowered, the examiner) decides specifically to terminate employment contracts. It is consistent with the policy of permitting the company to continue as a going concern that employees should be retained: the examiner is also encouraged to make as

---

4.   The application under section 9(4) must be made by the examiner on notice to the directors — see rule 11.
5.   Section 7(2).
6.   Section 5(2)(g), and section 5(4).
7.   Cf. *Donnelly v Gleeson*, High Court (unreported), 11 July 1978 (Hamilton J.).

much use of their services as he reasonably can in carrying out his tasks.[8] An examiner will regularly certify the wages of employees as an expense necessarily and properly incurred to avoid seriously prejudicing the survival of the company.[9]

Creditors of the Company

The prohibition on the exercise by creditors of the various remedies they may have against the company is the dramatic focal point of the legislation. Section 5 of the Act deals at length with the ways the exercise of these remedies are restricted. It is now proposed to examine the terms of the section in some detail.

Unsecured Creditors

Most unsecured creditors can normally only pursue recovery of their debt by instituting civil proceedings or by serving a statutory notice under section 214 of the Principal Act as a prerequisite to having the company wound up. Since no proceedings for the winding-up of a company may be commenced once the company is under court protection,[10] it is useless for a creditor to even present a winding up petition.[11] The court has power to grant leave to a party to commence proceedings against the company, subject to the various provisions of section 5(2),[12] but it is unlikely that such leave will be granted as of course. The creditor applying for leave will usually have to make out a case for him to be given such leave.[13] In deciding on this issue, the court will consider the interests of all concerned, including the legitimate interests of secured and unsecured creditors as well as the interests of the applicant.[14] But a number of other matters are likely to be considered relevant in this context: the probability and proportionality of benefit or loss to the various parties by the granting or refusal of leave, the conduct of the parties and the history and prospects of the examinership in question.[15] In particular, because of the emphasis of the Act on the survival

8.   Section 29(4).
9.   Section 10.
10.   Section 5(2)(a).
11.   But service of a demand under section 214 is probably not the commencement of proceedings.
12.   Section 5(3).
13.   *Re Atlantic Computer Systems (No. 1)* [1991] BCLC 606.
14.   *Royal Trust Bank v Buchler* [1989] BCLC 130.
15.   For a detailed analysis of the various principles which a court might consider, see *Atlantic Computer Systems (No. 1)* [1991] BCLC 606 at 632.

of the company and its undertaking as a going concern, any proceedings which might prejudice that survival are unlikely to be sanctioned. The court may also stay any proceedings already in existence against the company on the application of the examiner, or may make such other order as it thinks proper.[16] While again the Act does not state expressly the criteria which a court should bear in mind in deciding whether or not to stay existing proceedings, it is likely that considerations similar to those set out above will be relevant.[17] 'Proceedings' probably means legal proceedings or quasi-legal proceedings such as arbitration. To interpret the prohibition against 'proceedings' as meaning a prohibition against every sort of step which could be taken against the company, its contracts or its property has been held in England to be too wide.[18]

Secured Creditors

Any right of a secured creditor which may arise from a debenture held by him to appoint a receiver over some or all of the company's property or undertaking is removed by section 5(2)(b). As already indicated, a receiver already appointed will be unable to continue to act unless expressly permitted to do so under section 6. Unlike the UK legislation, the Act does not allow secured creditors to apply to court for leave to enforce their security created by a charge: only with the consent of the examiner can any action be taken to realise the whole or any part of such security.[19] While it might be possible for a secured creditor to apply to court under section 13(7) in respect of the examiner's decision if the examiner unreasonably withheld his consent, the Act seems to have specifically entrusted the power to grant or withhold leave to enforce such security to the examiner alone.

But the wording of section 5(2)(d) would appear to allow *some* creditors who hold security to realise that security without consent, depending on the nature of that security. Undoubtedly, a creditor whose claim is secured by a *charge* on the whole or any part of the property, effects, or income of the company requires the examiner's consent to take any action to realise that security. There is no statutory definition of 'charge' though the phrase appears wide enough to include fixed and floating charges as well as registered and unregistered charges under section 99 of the Principal Act. Other creditors whose claims are not secured by a charge may be able to

---

16. Section 5(3).
17. Applications should be on notice to company, examiner and other parties to the proceedings — rule 8.
18. *Bristol Airport plc v Powdrill* [1990] BCLC 585.
19. Section 5(2)(d).

enforce their security without the consent of the examiner. So, for example, a creditor claiming an unpaid vendor's lien may be able to assert his lien[20] or a landlord may be able to exercise his right of re-entry under a lease[21] without obtaining the prior consent of the examiner. It seems anomalous that such creditors should apparently be able to exercise their rights without even obtaining the leave of the court to do so. How this aspect of the law develops will depend on whether the court interprets the restriction as applying to *all* securities or only to claims secured by charge. But even if the broader restriction is preferred, there is still some doubt as to the steps a secured creditor may take. For example, will the registration of a judgment mortgage against the company's property count as an 'action taken to realise' the creditor's security? The answer would appear to be no, but redrafting would help to eliminate doubt.[22]

Leasing and Other Creditors

Other creditors may have supplied goods to the company on the basis of leasing agreements, hire-purchase agreements, credit sales agreements, retention of title agreements or even bailment agreements. As these creditors usually retain some interest or title in the goods supplied, they usually have an additional remedy not available to ordinary creditors: repossession. But it is clear that none of these creditors will be entitled to repossess (or even take steps to repossess) goods in the company's possession without the consent of the examiner once the protection period begins.[23] The issue of whether or not a finance company could repossess goods which had been leased to the company now under administration (which had in turn sub-leased them to end-users) from end-users was considered in *Re Atlantic Computer Systems (No. 1)*.[24] Accepting the difficulties in attempting to provide an exhaustive definition of 'possession',[25] the Court of Appeal approached the issue by looking at the purpose of the section. Since the objective appeared to be to protect goods from repossession unless consent is given, the court held that 'it is immaterial whether they remain on the company's premises, or are entrusted by the company to others for repair, or are sub-let by the company as part of its

20. *Re Sabre International* [1991] BCLC 470.
21. *Exchange Travel Ltd v Triton Property Trust* [1991] BCLC 397.
22. Section 11(3)(c) of the Insolvency Act in the UK provides that 'No . . . steps may be taken to enforce any security over the company's property. . . .'
23. Section 5(2)(d) and section 11(8).
24. [1991] BCLC 606.
25. See e.g. *Towers & Co. Ltd v Gray* [1961] 2 All ER 68.

trade to others'.[26] The goods in question were thus deemed to be in the possession of the company although physically present on the premises of the end-users. Again, there is no provision for application to the court for leave to repossess goods; the matter is solely within the discretion of the examiner.

Banking Creditors

A bank or other financial institution is not obliged to continue to advance monies to the company once the protection period has commenced. It may seek certification of advances from the examiner before making funds available or honouring cheques on an overdrawn account. However, a bank is not entitled to set-off (say) the deposit account of the company (which may be in credit) against the company's overdrawn current account unless the examiner consents.[27] 'Bank account' includes accounts with other financial institutions such as building, friendly and industrial provident societies as well as other institutions exempt from the licencing requirements of section 9 of the Central Bank Act 1971.

Even creditors who have obtained judgment against the company prior to the protection period are not allowed to put any such judgment into force by attachment, sequestration, distress or execution against the property of the company unless the examiner consents.[28] A sheriff is thus unable to seize the goods of a company under an order of *fieri facias*,[29] and a creditor may presumably be stopped from even obtaining such an order by the examiner under section 5(3).

Sureties and Indemnors

Some creditors will have obtained personal guarantees or indemnities from directors in respect of debts owed by the company. The Act prevents them from commencing proceedings or putting into force attachment, sequestration, distress or execution against any person 'liable to pay all or any part of the debts of the company under any enactment, rule of law or otherwise' or his property or effects.[30] This is an absolute bar — there is no discretion given to the examiner or the court to waive this prohibition. Again, it seems anomalous that an action against a guarantor of the debts

26.   At 623.
27.   Section 5(2)(h).
28.   Section 5(2)(c).
29.   *Re London and Devon Biscuits Co* [1871] 12 Eq. 190.
30.   Section 5(2)(f).

of the company can never be commenced while the company is under protection, even if little or no prejudice to the company's survival would be caused by such an action. Curiously, there is no prohibition against continuing with existing proceedings.

A creditor who acts in contravention of these restrictions is liable to be restrained from so doing by injunction and may face other sanctions, including an action for damages.[31] Nor is a creditor certain of being paid for the use which a company under protection may make of that creditor's property during the protection period unless it is certified as a necessary and proper expense at the time by the examiner; otherwise such a creditor's claim ranks as an unsecured debt of the company.

The prohibition of enforcement of various remedies is undoubtedly frustrating for creditors. It is strange that no facility to apply to court for leave to enforce remedies is available in most situations; the matter is left exclusively to the examiner. Perhaps it was thought that the relatively short duration of the protection period minimised any prejudice suffered by creditors in the interests of the company and its members and creditors as a whole. But a similar limit on the length of time that a company may remain under administration in the UK[32] has not prevented creditors from seeking to enforce their securities or taking other steps to protect their position in that jurisdiction. However, creditors who have secured or other proprietary rights are generally treated more favourably than unsecured creditors under the UK legislation; the Irish Act appears not to envisage any such preferential treatment for any particular class of creditors during the protection period.

Repudiation of Contracts

The appointment of an examiner does not alter the effect of pre-existing contracts: they remain binding on the company. The examiner will not be personally liable in respect of any such contracts unless he assumes the rights and obligations of the company under the contract by agreement with the company and the other contracting party under a novation.[33] He is personally liable for contracts entered into by him in his own name (or in

31.   A creditor who interfered with an administrator's possession of company property was held to be in contempt of court: *Bristol Airport Plc v Powdrill* [1990] BCLC 585.
32.   Under the UK legislation the administrator is obliged to report with proposals to creditors within three months of the making of the administration order, though this time can be extended.
33.   *Parsons v Sovereign Bank of Canada* [1913] AC 160.

the name of the company) in the performance of his functions unless the contract provides otherwise. But the company may also wish to affirm or repudiate existing contracts. Section 20 provides a mechanism for this process. Subject to the approval of the court, the company may affirm or repudiate any contract under which some element of performance other than payment remains to be rendered by both the company and the other contracting party. On hearing the application (which should be on notice to the examiner and to any person suffering loss or damage as a result of such repudiation),[34] the court may also make an order determining the amount of loss or damage suffered by the other party; that amount will then be due as a judgment debt by the company to that party, who ranks as an unsecured creditor. The court may make such other order as it sees fit, including orders as to notice to, or declaring the rights of, any party affected by the affirmation or repudiation. This means that where necessary the court's order can deal with the rights and liabilities of persons who are not parties to the contract.[35] Effectively this is a simplified version of the power given to a liquidator in section 290 of the Principal Act to disclaim onerous contracts. But the power to affirm or repudiate can only arise where proposals for a compromise or scheme of arrangement are to be formulated: the determination by the court of the amount of loss or damage suffered thus helps to fix the amount due to a creditor who is presumably then accorded the appropriate voting rights and dividend at the meetings of creditors. Determining the amount due also helps to give the court a clear picture of the liabilities of the company at the hearing to consider the examiner's proposals. It is not clear how early in the examinership the company would be entitled to apply, but the examiner is likely to have completed his first report on the viability of the company before such an application is made.

The purpose of the section is to allow the company to dispose of agreements which are unprofitable or unduly onerous. It may also be a prelude to the company 'hiving down' its undertaking so as to concentrate only on the viable aspects of the company's business while disposing of those parts which are uneconomic or ineffective. The section performs an important function, since it would appear that an examiner might not otherwise be able to act in contravention of the terms of a pre-existing agreement made by the company.[36]

---

34.   Section 20(4) — see rule 19.
35.   See *Tempany v Royal Liver Co* [1984)] I.L.R.M. 273, followed in *Re GWI Ltd*, High Court (unreported), 16 November 1988 (Murphy J.).
36.   See *Astor Chemicals v Synthetic Technology* [1990] BCLC 1.

Company Property

The start of court protection has no automatic effect on property owned by the company: the title remains unaffected and does not vest in the examiner or anyone else. While there is no statutory definition of what constitutes company property, it has been held to include a company's interest in goods held by it under chattel leases[37] and may even include other goods or land in which the company has some form of legal or equitable interest although this definition contained in the UK legislation is extraordinarily wide.

It may be anticipated that a landlord or other lessor will attempt to provide in the terms of his lease for re-entry into, or repossession of, his premises or goods in the event of the company going into examinership, but the exercise of any such right is likely to be curtailed by the provisions of section 5.

---

37. *Bristol Airport v Powdrill* [1990] BCLC 585 (leased aircraft).

CHAPTER 4

Functions and Powers of the Examiner

The principal function of the examiner is to investigate the viability of the company and, where appropriate, to formulate proposals for a survival scheme for presentation to the members and creditors, and ultimately to the court. Unlike an administrator appointed under the UK legislation, he is not an officer of the company and has no power to manage the business of the company unless expressly permitted to do so by the court.[1] As will be seen, however, the examiner is given a wide range of powers to assist him in carrying out his primary obligation. The legislation also permits the court to grant further powers to the examiner where necessary.

Examination of the Company's Affairs

Usually what an examiner will require most urgently is information about the company. To some extent this will be provided by the statement of affairs which the directors must submit to him within seven days of his appointment.[2] But this may not be enough, particularly if the examiner wishes to investigate further any suspicion of reckless or fraudulent trading. He is thus given power to compel all officers and agents of the company (or related companies) to give him all assistance in connection with his functions which they are reasonably able to give. This may mean requiring them to attend before him and to produce all books and documents of, or relating to, that company.[3] In this respect, it is noteworthy that section 244A of the Principal Act (as amended by section 125 of the Companies Act 1990) prevents any person from withholding possession of any deed, document or papers belonging to the company or relating to the company's affairs from the examiner. Nor is any such person entitled to refuse to produce such

1. A number of decisions have stressed that the office of examiner is essentially advisory rather than executive in nature. See *Re Bernard McDevitt & Co.*, High Court (unreported), 9 July 1993 and *Re Edenpark Construction Ltd*, High Court (unreported), 17 December 1993 (both Murphy J). Cf. *Re Home Treat Ltd* [1991] BCLC 705.
2. Section 14.   3. Section 8(1).

documents even if they claim a lien or some other form of security by virtue of the deposit of the documents with them, though production of the documentation to the examiner is deemed to be 'without prejudice' to that person's rights under the mortgage, charge or pledge. He may also require persons other than officers or agents of the company to assist him if necessary; employees, shareholders and others may thus be required to attend.[4] He is also empowered to examine these persons on oath (orally, or by way of written interrogatories) in relation to the company's affairs. While persons so questioned or required to produce information may refuse to comply on the grounds of legal professional privilege,[5] it is clear that such persons could prejudice their own position if forced to answer all questions put to them. However, the section does not appear to be as oppressive as section 245 of the Principal Act (which expressly denies persons the right to refuse to answer on grounds of incrimination).[6] A person who refuses to produce the required documentation or refuses to attend or answer questions faces an enquiry by the court into the case, though the power to punish such a person as if he had been guilty of contempt of court has been held to be unconstitutional in *Desmond v Glackin*.[6a] He may be ordered to re-attend before the examiner, but he may also be excused by direction of the court from providing certain documents or answering particular questions.[7] In adjudicating on whether a person should be compelled to answer certain questions, it is likely that the court will attempt to balance the importance of the information to the examiner for the carrying out of his functions with the possible oppression which may be caused to the person being examined. While it is unlikely that an examiner will be permitted to use the opportunity to investigate the defence which an officer has to a claim which the examiner has decided to commence against him, the court is likely to allow the examiner to seek as much information as would be necessary to reconstitute the state of knowledge which the company itself should possess.[8] It may be less likely that such orders will be made against third parties, and an order for oral examination is usually viewed as being more oppressive than an order for the production of documents. Any such enquiry by the examiner is undoubtedly subject to the

4.   'Officers' and 'agents' include past as well as present officers and agents. 'Agents' includes bankers, solicitors and auditors of the company — section 8(6).
5.   Section 8(5B), applying section 23(1)(5) of the Companies Act 1990.
6.   At sub-section (6).
6a.   Supreme Court (unreported) 30 July 1992 (considering the same power contained in section 10(5) of the Companies Act 1990).
7.   Section 8(5) and (5A).
8.   See *Cloverbay v BCCI* [1991] BCLC 135 at 141.

constitutionally-guaranteed principles of natural justice.

Many of the powers thus given to the examiner are similar to those given to auditors[9] and inspectors appointed to investigate the company's affairs. For example, the examiner is also given power to require directors to produce documents relating to bank accounts which may have been used for undisclosed company transactions or improper acts or omissions connected with the company.[10]

Powers Relating to the Continuance of Business by the Company

While the examiner does not take over the business of the company, he is certainly given an opportunity to influence management decisions. He can convene, set the agenda for, and preside at meetings of directors and of members, as well as presenting reports and proposing resolutions to such meetings. He is also entitled to reasonable notice of any board meetings or general meetings.[11] But he is also allowed to intervene in the conduct of the business of the company if he believes it necessary to avoid prejudice to the position of the company or another party. Section 7(5) gives the examiner an extremely wide power to take whatever steps are necessary to halt, prevent or rectify the effects of any act or omission or conduct, decision or contract relating to the income, assets or liabilities which in his opinion is, or is likely to be, detrimental to the company or any interested party. He must, however, consider the rights of any person who in good faith and for value acquired an interest in the income, assets or liabilities in question, as any action which he takes will be subject to those rights. The section could thus permit an examiner, to, for example, prevent a contract for the sale of company property from going ahead, though presumably the other contracting party would not be denied the right to pursue a claim in damages[12] against the company. How exactly this section will be used is of considerable interest; it provides extremely wide powers of intervention for the examiner.

Ultimately the examiner may be given some or all of the powers and functions vested in the directors if the court feels it is just and equitable to do so.[13] Clearly this gives an extremely wide discretion to the court, though in considering whether or not to make such an order the court must consider:

(a) whether the affairs of the company are (or are likely to be)

9.   Section 7(1). See also section 193(3) of Companies Act 1990.
10.   Section 8(3). See section 10 of the Companies Act 1990.
11.   Section 7(2) and (3).
12.   Though, arguably, not a claim for specific performance.
13.   Section 9.

conducted in a way calculated or likely to prejudice the interests of the company or its employees or its creditors as a whole,[14] or

(b) whether it is expedient to curtail or regulate the exercise of powers or the carrying on of business by the directors or management in order to preserve the assets or safeguard the interests of the company, employees or creditors,[15] or

(c) that the company (or its directors) have resolved that such an order shall be made.[16]

The court can consider any other relevant matter relating to the company and in making the order it may include conditions or ancillary orders as it sees fit. So far the court has rarely been requested by the examiner to grant him such powers.

The Act certainly permits the examiner to be in a position to actually manage the business of the company. He may also be given by court order all or any of the powers a court-appointed liquidator would have.[17] Such an order would allow him to exercise a number of powers and functions without the necessity for prior court approval.[18] It is submitted, however, that in general an examiner is unlikely to become involved in the management of the company, concentrating instead on exploring its future prospects. The Act seems to permit rather than to exhort active participation by the examiner in the company business.

Many of the functions exercisable by the examiner are exercisable by him only at the direction or with the prior sanction of the court. For example, the examiner may be directed to ascertain and agree claims against the company.[19] This obviously assists the examiner (and, ultimately, the court) in deciding on the nature and extent of the various liabilities of the company. The examiner will usually seek prior approval before exercising other powers not expressly conferred on him, such as disclaiming onerous property or contracts of the company. Analogous to the power to disclaim onerous property or contracts is the power granted under section 11 permitting the examiner (where so authorised by the court) to dispose or otherwise deal with property or goods even where they may be subject to a charge, hire-purchase agreement or other similar arrangement. Before

14. Section 9(2)(a).   15. Section 9(2)(b).
16. Section 9(2)(c).   17. Section 9(4).
18. Section 231(2) of the Principal Act.
19. Section 7(7). Unless so directed, he should not adjudicate on such claims; if there are real grounds for dispute, these claims can be put in a separate class in any scheme of arrangement, written down accordingly and adjudicated upon at a later date. See *Wogan's (Drogheda) Ltd (No. 3)*, High Court (unreported), 9 February 1993 (Costello J.).

allowing an examiner to deal with property in this way, the court must be satisfied that the disposal would be likely to facilitate the whole or any part of the company as a going concern.[20] The examiner may thus be empowered to dispose of or exercise powers in respect of:

> (i) company property the subject of a floating charge,
> (ii) company property which is subject to other securities (e.g. fixed charge, lien),
> (iii) goods in the possession of the company under hire-purchase, conditional sale, retention of title and certain bailment agreements.[21]

But the section does not mean that security-holders lose all rights and priorities. Such secured creditors will be entitled to the same priority over the proceeds of the property disposed of as they would have had in respect of the original property. It is also clear that any shortfall between the proceeds obtained and the open market value of the property must be made up from the assets of the company in order to discharge the sum secured or payable under the hire-purchase agreement. So an examiner who sells premises belonging to the company over which a creditor holds, for example, a floating charge must apply:

> (a) the net proceeds of the sale, and
> (b) where there is a deficiency, the difference between the net proceeds and the net amount which the court determines would have been realized on a sale of the property on the open market by a willing vendor[22]

towards discharge of the sum secured or payable.

This is an intriguing provision. It is similar in many respects to section 15 of the UK Insolvency Act 1986. It allows the examiner to hive off property or goods where to continue to retain them would be uneconomic and would seriously prejudice the company's prospect of survival, while preserving any rights that secured or similar creditors may have in respect of that property. Examples would include buildings incurring substantial overheads or chattels[23] leased to the company which no longer needed be retained to ensure the survival of the company. But the section raises a number of complex issues, some of which have been addressed in case law

---

20.   Section 11(2). The application of the examiner should be made on notice to the holder of any security or the hire-purchase company or any other person appearing to have an interest in the property — rule 12.
21.   Section 11(8).   22. Section 11(4).
23.   E.g. company cars or non-essential equipment.

on the equivalent section in the UK legislation. In *ARV Aviation Ltd*[24] administrators wished to sell the company's business which was subject to a fixed charge in favour of two creditors. One of these secured creditors opposed the granting of court sanction for such a sale. In the course of the hearing a dispute arose as to the valuation of the assets to be sold, the secured creditor suggesting that the value of the assets over which they held a secured charge was less than that contended for by the administrators. The question of valuation is important since it is clear that if the net proceeds of the disposal are less than the amount which would have been realised by a sale on the open market by a willing vendor additional funds must be provided from the company's assets to make good that deficiency. Obviously such a step could diminish the funds available to other (e.g. unsecured) creditors. The unsecured creditors unanimously supported the proposed sale.

Knox J. held that the court must balance the prejudice which might be suffered by the secured creditor if the sale was allowed against the prejudice that would be felt by others interested in the outcome of the administration (in Irish terms, the survival of the company in whole or in part as a going concern) if the sale was prevented. In order to establish exactly what the second creditor is entitled to, he suggested that a two-stage procedure be adopted. Firstly, valuations should be submitted to the court: then, if the matter is still in dispute, the court may direct an enquiry as to the value of the property if sold 'on the open market by a willing vendor'. This is an expression which is extremely difficult to define. If the company wishes that property be sold to facilitate the company's survival and actively seeks a purchaser, is this not a sale on the open market by a willing vendor? Does the insolvency of that company make it any less 'willing' as a vendor? Perhaps the fact that the company is forced to sell in order to survive may be interpreted as making it less 'willing'. The concept of the 'open market' value of property is not without difficulty in this context either: does a sale to secure the survival of a company take place on a more or less 'open' market than a sale by a receiver or liquidator, or a company not in examinership? The court did not expressly decide the point. In *ARV Aviation* it was held that it was intended that the rights of a secured creditor should be protected to the maximum practicable extent, and therefore that the 'open market/willing vendor' value would be not less than what one would anticipate a secured creditor himself could realise.

Since the net proceeds (and, where necessary, additional monies) equivalent to the 'open market/willing vendor' value must be applied

24.   [1989] BCLC 665

towards discharging the sums secured by the security (or payable under the hire-purchase agreement), it is important to ascertain what those sums are. In *ARV Aviation* the court defined 'the sums secured by the security' as covering the capital sum originally secured, interest properly payable thereunder and costs which the secured creditor is entitled to add by law or under the instrument itself (including the costs of proceedings connected with the realisation or otherwise, subject to the court's general discretion as to costs).[25]

Whether examiners will use this mechanism regularly remains to be seen; it has not been used to date in this jurisdiction. Given the time-scale envisaged by the Act, it is perhaps more likely that a sale of secured property and the consequences thereof would be incorporated as part of proposals for a scheme of arrangement rather than made the subject of a separate application to court. Aside from any administrative convenience, the examiner may also wish to consider challenging the validity of the security in question; the proceeds of sale of the secured property will not necessarily be put 'on ice' pending the examiner's decision on this matter.[26]

Power of Certification

The power of certification given by the Act to the examiner is probably the most dramatic and controversial power which he can exercise. The purpose of the section is to permit an examiner to reassure creditors with whom the company must continue to trade during the protection period that they will be paid for the necessary goods and services supplied to the company during the protection period. By a combination of section 10 and section 29, expenses certified by the examiner under section 10 are given priority (along with the remuneration and legal costs of the examiner) over all other debts owed by the company, unless otherwise directed by the court. Thus, creditors who would normally be unsecured (e.g. trade creditors) can obtain priority and payment ahead of secured and preferential creditors for the services provided by them to the company during the protection period. This statutory 'leap-frogging' of priority of debt has been severely criticised, notably by secured creditors who find themselves passed over.

The aim of the section is laudable: a company which is admittedly insolvent would have little or no chance of obtaining credit or goods and services during the protection period otherwise. This would seriously prejudice the survival of most companies as a going concern; certification can thus give comfort to creditors who continue to supply to the company.

25.   At 669.
26.   *Re Newman Shopfitters Ltd* [1991] BCLC 407.

The effect of certification is so dramatic, however, that the criteria set out in section 10 should be rigidly adhered to by any examiner. As pointed out in *Re Don Bluth Entertainment Ltd (No. 2)*,[27] great care and professional expertise should be exercised by an examiner in issuing certificates under section 10.

Firstly, an examiner would be wise to ask the directors of the company under court protection to submit proposals (preferably in writing) in respect of particular liabilities which the company proposes to incur during the protection period. He should also ask for details of how the incurring of these liabilities would benefit the company, and in particular how these liabilities would contribute to the survival of the company during the protection period.

Having gathered this information, the examiner can then decide what (if any) liabilities of the company during the protection period should be certified. In deciding whether or not to issue a certificate for a particular liability, he should consider whether the company's survival as a *going concern* during the protection period would otherwise be seriously prejudiced. The examiner can only issue a certificate in respect of a liability actually incurred during the protection period; an invoice which arrives at the company during the protection period in respect of works carried out before is not certifiable. Furthermore, the examiner should endeavour to ensure that the certificate is issued at the time the liability is incurred, i.e. contemporaneously, or as soon as possible thereafter, though a hiatus or delay may in certain circumstances be inevitable.[28]

The examiner should also ensure that the certificate given is valid on its face. No form for the certificate is provided in the legislation or the rules, but ideally the certificate should:

> (i) be issued in writing. While there is no legislative requirement that the certificate be in writing (and in certain extreme circumstances oral certification has been permitted),[29] the view has been expressed that this is an obvious and inescapable administrative necessity,[29a]

---

27.   High Court (unreported), 24 May 1993 (Murphy J.). In *Re Edenpark Construction Ltd*, High Court (unreported) 17 December 1993 (Murphy J.) there is a further detailed analysis of this responsibility of the examiner.

28.   *Re Atlantic Magnetics (No. 2)*, High Court (unreported), 4 May 1992 (Murphy J.) (*ex tempore*).

29.   In the UMP examinership, oral certification was provided to some creditors.

29a. *Re Edenpark Construction Ltd*, High Court (unreported), 17 December 1993 (Murphy J.).

(ii) be dated,

(iii)indicate that the priority granted to the amount certified is subject to there being assets of the company available to discharge it,

(iv) identify the particular goods or services to be supplied and certified,

(v) indicate the extent of the liability certified,

(vi) indicate that the liability certified is and remains that of the *company* and not of the examiner personally, and

(vii) explain why the liability is being certified and the consequences of certification under section 10.

The examiner would be wise to keep all documentation relating to proposals and certification.

In addition to the limits expressed or implicit in section 10, section 29 allows the court to make such orders as it sees fit for the payment of the reasonable expenses properly incurred by the examiner. While this jurisdiction is not usually invoked until a final application is made by the examiner for payment of his remuneration, costs and expenses, it has been held to confer a discretion on the court at a much earlier stage in the examinership. In *Re Don Bluth Entertainment (No. 1)*,[30] Murphy J. limited the liabilities which could be sanctioned by the court to a specific sum. He also ordered that the liabilities certified henceforth should be limited to liabilities incurred by the company (presumably by way of borrowings) to a particular bank which had provided extensive funding in the past to the company (and which had opposed the petition) or such other bank or institution as the court might approve. In this way the bank was given the first opportunity to avail of the special priority granted by the certification procedure. Such limitation could help to allay fears that secured creditors could be 'passed out' by other creditors who provided goods or services under certificates for vast amounts of money without first being given the option of lending the money under a certificate themselves. The difficulty with the procedure is, however, that certification of a protection period liability will be at the expense of secured creditors unless the rescue package is sufficient to discharge all secured debts in full. If the examinership fails, the certification process may also affect other trade creditors since the combination of the 'certified' creditors and secured creditors may mean that no dividend is available for the unsecured creditors. Examiners should thus restrict the liabilities certified by them only to goods and services which are absolutely essential to the company's survival as a going concern during

30.   High Court (unreported), 27 August 1992.

the protection period. The power of the court to review certificates will be dealt with in Chapter 10.

In addition, it seems that a creditor or interested party could object to the exercise by the examiner of his power of certification by applying to the court under section 13(7).

Powers of Examiner in respect of Improper Transactions or Behaviour

The power of an examiner to prevent a company from carrying out a course of conduct which might be detrimental has already been discussed. But an examiner can also take corrective action to restore to the company property which had been disposed of in such a way as to perpetrate a fraud on the company, creditors or members. Section 139 of the Companies Act 1990[31] gives the court power to order any person who has the use, control or possession of such property or sale proceeds to restore them (or pay an equivalent sum) to the examiner on such terms as it sees fit. The application is made by the examiner (or a contributory or creditor) who must satisfy the court that it is just and equitable to make such an order. In deciding whether to grant the order, the court must have regard for the rights of *bona fide* purchasers for value of any interest in the property in question. While this section primarily supplements the power of a liquidator to set aside an earlier transaction by the company as being a fraudulent preference[32] under section 286(1) of the Principal Act, it can clearly be used by an examiner to recover property improperly disposed of, thereby swelling the assets of the company available to creditors under a scheme of arrangement.

The examiner is also empowered under section 297A of the Principal Act as amended to apply to the court for a declaration that an officer of the company should be held personally liable for the debts of the company, having been guilty of fraudulent or reckless trading. The concepts of fraudulent and reckless trading will be discussed in Chapter 9. The usefulness of this power to an examiner is somewhat limited since the court may only grant a declaration in respect of an officer party to reckless trading if the applicant can show that he has suffered loss or damage as a consequence of that behaviour. It is hard to see how an examiner could show loss or damage to himself since no action for reckless trading will lie in respect of the behaviour of the company's officers during the period of court protection. However, no such requirement of personal loss or damage on

---

31.   Which applies to examiners by section 180(2) of the same Act.
32.   The procedure does not apply to 'fraudulent preferences' under section 286(1) — see section 139(2).

the part of the examiner is required in respect of a declaration of fraudulent trading by an officer of the company. It is hard in practice to reconcile the right of an examiner, or indeed a creditor, to bring such proceedings with the process of court protection. The practical difficulties were examined by Murphy J. in *Re Hefferon Kearns Ltd*.[33] Firstly, any such proceedings would almost certainly require a plenary hearing, with pleadings, discovery and detailed expert examination of the books and records of the company being necessary prior to any such hearing. Such pre-trial delays would almost certainly exceed the time scale envisaged by the Act during which a company could remain under court protection; and even if the protection order was to be continued until the proceedings were concluded, this could result in considerable injustice to creditors, who would still be unable to institute proceedings or execute against the company.

Secondly, while section 5(2)(f) does not prevent proceedings being instituted against the officers of a company in respect of a *potential* liability which they might have for the debts of the company, once the court finds that the officers *are* liable under section 297A, the provisions of section 5(2)(f) mean that no execution can be levied against those officers while the company remains under court protection.

In addition, it has also been pointed out[34] that even a successful creditor would not necessarily derive any benefit from the proceedings if a court were subsequently to sanction a scheme of arrangement, since the terms of the scheme would limit the dividend available. So it seems that the only circumstances in which a creditor could derive a benefit would be by instituting proceedings during the period of court protection and then implementing the judgment of the court if and when the scheme proposed by the examiner was rejected. It is difficult to disagree with the view that proceedings under section 297A can only operate effectively in the context of an insolvent liquidation. The likely consequence of utilising the procedure during an examinership would be to prejudice if not defeat the prospects of salvaging the business of the company.[35]

In the event of any examiner wishing to institute such proceedings, he would be wise to obtain the prior leave of the court; otherwise he may find himself personally bearing the costs of instituting and maintaining the proceedings (including, in the event of defeat, any order for costs made

33. *Re Hefferon Kearns Ltd — Dublin Heating Co Ltd v Hefferon and Others* [1992] ILRM 51.

34. McCann, 'Reckless trading; no looking back', 1992 10 ILT (n.s.) 61.

35. In *Re Hefferon Kearns*, the court refused to sanction a proposed scheme of arrangement because of outstanding proceedings under section 297A. Although the proceedings were unsuccessful, the examinership failed and the company was subsequently placed in liquidation.

against him). Indeed, in *Re Wogans (Drogheda) Ltd (No. 3)*[36] Costello J. expressed the view that an examiner should not institute *any* proceedings without first obtaining leave of the court under section 7(6) 'save in exceptional circumstances of urgency'.[37] If prior court sanction is obtained, the examiner should have no difficulty in being allowed the costs incurred as a priority payment under section 29 of the Act, even if the proceedings are ultimately unsuccessful.

Appointment, Removal and Other Provisions

Section 28(1) provides that a person will not be qualified to be appointed or act as an examiner if he would not be qualified to act as liquidator of that company. This means that persons who were officers or servants of the company within 12 months of the beginning of protection, and persons who are partners, employees or certain close relations of an officer of the company are excluded by virtue of the provision of sections 300 and 300A of the Principal Act. Bodies corporate are likewise disqualified.[38] The accountancy profession has specific guidelines which may also prevent persons acting if they have had an ongoing professional relationship with the company prior to their appointment. The independent status of the examiner is significant; as pointed out by Costello J. in *Re Wogans (Drogheda) Ltd (No. 3)*,[39] an examiner appointed by the court must be impartial between the the company's shareholders and its creditors, and the court will be very slow to appoint an accountant previously associated with the company. Any person nominated for appointment should consider this matter seriously. He, as well as the company's professional advisers, has a duty to exercise good faith to the court, and in particular to take reasonable steps to ensure that the court is not misled. In *Re Wogans (Drogheda) Ltd (No. 3)* the court had refused to appoint an examiner on an interim basis. However, the nominee had provided services to the company up to the date of hearing of the petition and had been paid for this. The examiner was also aware of irregularities and inaccuracies contained in the statement of affairs prior to the hearing of the petition. It was held that his failure to inform the court of his prior involvement with the company, and of the irregularities and inaccuracies relating to the statement of affairs, was a breach of his duty to the court. The court also held that this breach, in the circumstances,

36. High Court (unreported), 9 February 1993 (Costello J.).
37. At page 32 of the judgment.
38. The penalty for acting as an examiner while disqualified is a fine — section 28(2). The acts of an examiner remain valid even though defects are afterwards discovered in his appointment or qualification — section 13(5).
39. See footnote 36 above (at page 14).

disentitled him to payment of remuneration, costs or expenses incurred by him in the course of the examinership. The decision is a warning to all professional persons of the impartiality and responsibility required of anyone nominated to act as examiner.

The examiner may resign, or on cause shown, be removed by the court.[40] Questions of the impartiality and *bona fides* of the examiner will usually be resolved at the hearing of the petition, and it is unlikely that an examiner will subsequently be removed without compelling reasons. A general power is given to the company or any interested party to apply to the court in respect of the performance (or otherwise) by the examiner of his functions.[41] This seems wide enough to cover most queries which might arise. Unlike the UK legislation, there is no statutory power to compel the examiner to pay compensation for managing the company's affairs in a manner unfairly prejudicial to the creditors.[42] There seems no reason, however, why an examiner should not be required to meet the same standards and duty of care of ordinary skilled insolvency practitioners;[43] no immunity from liability for tort or misfeasance is given to him by the Act. Any vacancy in the office of examiner may be filled by the court.

An examiner may wish (or may be so directed by the court) to appoint a creditors' committee. This may be of particular help to him where there are a very large number of creditors. The committee will usually consist of not more than five members, three of whom should be the largest unsecured creditors willing to serve.[44] Such a committee may help an examiner in formulating an acceptable scheme of arrangement as well as giving other practical advice. The committee must be given copies of any proposals for such a scheme and may express a view thereon on its own behalf or on behalf of the classes of creditors it represents.

The personal liability of an examiner for any contract entered into by him in the performance of his functions has already been referred to.[45] This liability exists even if the contract is entered into by him in the name of the company, and an examiner should take care to ensure that the terms of the contract expressly provide that he is not to be personally liable where this is desired. The examiner is entitled to an indemnity from the company in respect of any personal liability on such a contract, though as no provision is made for the priority of payment of such an indemnity under section 29, this indemnity may often be worthless. It is also provided that he will not be entitled to any indemnity in respect of contracts entered into 'without

---

40.   Section 13(1).   41. Section 13(7).
42.   Section 27 of the UK Act.
43.   See *Re Charnley Davies Ltd (No. 2)* [1990] BCLC 760.
44.   Section 21(2).   45. Section 13(6).

authority'; this appears to refer to contracts which go outside or beyond the performance of his functions, though the meaning is not entirely clear.

The examiner is obliged to ensure that orders, made by the court in connection with his functions are given appropriate publicity. As well as delivering copies of the order relating to his appointment to the Registrar of Companies, he must publish his appointment in *Iris Oifigiúil* and any two newspapers.[46] He must also ensure that orders under sections 11, 17 and 24 are delivered to the Registrar of Companies, and consequent publication of this, in *Iris Oifigiúil* is required in some cases also.[47] The penalty for failure to comply with the requirement relating to publicity (proceedings in respect of which may be instituted by the Registrar of Companies) is a fine.[48]

Remuneration

The examiner is entitled to be remunerated for work done by him on behalf of the company. Payment of this remuneration will normally be made only after the court has sanctioned it under section 29. In determining the entitlement of the examiner to remuneration, the court will take into account the extent to which the examiner has made use of the services of the staff and facilities of the company, since the examiner should make such use so far as is reasonably possible to assist him in performing his function.[49] The court may also consider whether unnecessary additional staff have been recruited resulting in additional costs, and may enquire as it sees fit into the nature of work done and the level of remuneration claimed. An examiner who has acted for a period outside the scope of the authority given to him by the Act may be disentitled to remuneration for that period.[50] Similar considerations apply to the legal costs incurred by the examiner during the protection period.

46. Section 12.
47. Section 30.
48. Section 30; section 36A.
49. Section 29(4).
50. See *Re Clare Textiles Ltd (in liquidation)* [1993] 2 IR 213. See also chapter 10.

CHAPTER 5

First Report of the Examiner

The first statutory obligation imposed on an examiner is the duty to conduct an examination of the company's affairs and report thereon to the court. It is clear from section 15 that (unless additional time is given by the court) this report must be furnished to the court within 21 days of his appointment. This is another example of the extremely short time period of protection envisaged by the legislation. Since an interim examiner may be appointed on the day the petition is presented, this time may start to run from the very day protection begins. While the Act makes no provision for the appointment of an interim examiner, it is submitted that time could begin to run from the date of appointment of an interim examiner, given the gravity of the time frame contained in the Act. The time can be extended if, for example, a new examiner is appointed at the hearing of the petition, or if the court otherwise sees fit.[1]

The examiner is helped in the performance of his task by the number of obligations imposed on the directors and officers of the company. Directors are obliged (within seven days of his appointment) to submit a statement of affairs.[2] This must show (so far as is reasonably possible) the company's assets, liabilities and debts, as well as information about creditors and their securities (if any). The court can also direct that further information be provided.[3] Directors may also be required to produce documents relating to personal bank accounts.[4] In addition, the examiner can direct all officers and agents of the company (or a related company) to provide all books and documents relating to the company, as well as requiring them to attend before him and to assist generally.[5] An examiner may make similar directions and requirements of any other person he considers to be in possession of information concerning the affairs of the company.[6] As already explained, these are extremely wide-ranging and effective powers,

1. Section 15(1).
2. Section 14(1).
3. Section 14(2).
4. Section 8(3).
5. Section 8(1).
6. Section 8(2).

designed to help the examiner obtain as much relevant information as possible.

Contents of the Report

The report may be extremely brief, perhaps because the examiner has been unable to obtain sufficient information. The Act requires, however, that certain specific matters be dealt with in the report.[7] These will now be examined in detail.

(a) The names of the permanent addresses of the officers of the company, and, in so far as the examiner can establish, any person in accordance with whose directions and instructions the directors of the company are accustomed to act.
This includes directors, the company secretary and auditors of the company. The examiner is also obliged to report any 'shadow director' of the company. While the issue of whether a person is to be regarded as a shadow director is to some extent a matter of degree, if an examiner is satisfied (so far as he can establish) as to the existence of such a person, the name and address should be included in the report. If the evidence to date suggests that no such 'shadow director' exists, he should say so.

(b) The names of any other bodies corporate of which the directors of the company are also directors.
These may or may not include related companies.

(c) A statement as to the affairs of the company showing, so far as is reasonably possible to do so, particulars of the company's assets, debts and liabilities (including contingent and prospective liabilities) as of the latest practicable date, the names and address of its creditors, the securities held by them respectively and the dates that the securities were given.
Again, the obligation on the examiner is to give a financial picture of the company in so far as is reasonably possible. Hence the requirement that the assets, debts and liabilities be shown as they were at the latest practicable date. Preferably the report should set out the fixed and current assets, and the secured, preferential and various other creditors. It may be of considerable help to show the projected outcome if the company were to survive as a going concern, and to contrast that with the estimated outcome if the

7.   Section 16.

company were to be wound-up (or, perhaps, if the principal assets were sold by a receiver in a receivership). Ideally, the examiner should also endeavour to list the creditors (and debtors) of the company, perhaps by way of an appendix.

(d) Whether in the opinion of the examiner any deficiency between the assets and the liabilities of the company has been satisfactorily accounted for or, if not, whether there is evidence of a substantial disappearance of property that is not adequately accounted for.

In some companies a deficiency between the assets and liabilities may only be apparent if assets are valued on a break-up basis rather than on a going concern basis. This difference should be explained, perhaps by reference to the nature of the assets themselves. Many companies will be in a position where the liabilities exceed assets on any valuation. The examiner should attempt to show how this deficiency arose. A number of factors may be relevant: bad management and business practices, losses of subsidiary or associated companies, and so on. The examiner is not obliged to justify the deficiency, but rather to establish whether or not there has been any impropriety or irregularity, and if he is aware of any such matters he should advert to them. Any evidence suggesting a substantial disappearance of property must also be reported if no acceptable explanation has been given to him. Any such disappearance should obviously be investigated as thoroughly as possible by the examiner.

(e) A statement of opinion by the examiner as to whether the company, and the whole or any part of its undertaking, would be capable of survival as a going concern and a statement of the conditions which he feels are essential to ensure such survival, whether as regards the internal management and controls of the company or otherwise.

This is the first occasion on which a statutory obligation is imposed on the examiner to express a view on the future viability of the company and its business. In formulating this view, a number of points should be noted.

Firstly, the examiner must consider the capability of the company for survival as a going concern *and* the whole or part of its undertaking. Only if such a conclusion is reached by him does the Act permit him to formulate proposals for a scheme of arrangement. So it will not be sufficient to suggest that the company (e.g. its name or goodwill) could be preserved but that the business itself will fail. Nor will it be appropriate to allow the examination to go further if the examiner expresses the view that the company's undertaking or business in its entirety should be sold. Such a sale (even on a going concern basis) is more properly the function of a liquidator. The purpose of the Act is to examine whether the company *and its business together* (in whole or part) can survive.[8]

'Undertaking' is not defined within the Act, but can be understood to mean the enterprise or business of the company.

Secondly, it is clear that while some of the undertaking may have to be sold on a break-up basis, at least part must be capable of survival as a going concern if the examination process is to continue. The examiner should try (so far as possible) to identify that part of the business which he thinks capable of survival, and to explain why he is of this view. He may be able to point to work-in-progress, orders received, financial statements or other matters of relevance in coming to this conclusion.

But some adjustment of the company's position will usually be necessary, and so the examiner must expressly state what are the essential conditions required to ensure the survival of the company and its business. For example, the company may need to enter into a compromise or restructuring of its debts with some or all of its creditors. Additional finance, whether by investment or the issue of additional share capital, will almost always be required. Certain business practices may have to be altered or discontinued. In particular, the internal management structure may require revision. A company may require the imposition of tighter financial controls or an updated system of book-keeping. In suggesting that an alteration to the internal management and controls of the company could be a condition necessary for survival, the section appears to recognise common difficulties within companies in financial trouble.

(f) His opinion as to whether the formulation, acceptance and confirmation of proposals for a compromise or scheme of arrangements would facilitate such survival.

If the examiner has already expressed the view (above) that the company and its business are capable of survival as a going concern (subject to whatever condition he may suggest), it is likely that he will be of the view that the proposal and implementation of a scheme of arrangement[9] as described will assist or facilitate the company's survival. In the absence of any prospect of survival, an examiner should state that such steps appear to be pointless.

8. *Re Clare Textiles Ltd (in liquidation)* [1993] 2 IR 213.
9. 'Compromise' and 'scheme of arrangement' are not defined. See below chapter 6.

(g) Whether, in his opinion, an attempt to continue the whole or any part of the undertaking of the company would be likely to be more advantageous to the members as a whole and the creditors as a whole, than a winding-up.
Since the purpose of the Act is to examine and provide for the survival of ailing companies where possible, it is clearly important to know whether the winding-up of a company is likely to be more beneficial to the members and creditors than continuing the company's business. In expressing his view on this point, the examiner should remember to consider the position of the members *as a whole* and the creditors *as a whole*. So, simply because a particular class of shareholders may be subject to calls if the company was wound-up does not lead to the conclusion that liquidation would be less advantageous to the members as a whole; all classes must be considered. Similarly, the fact that certain preferential or secured creditors would be paid in full in a winding-up is not of critical importance if the best interests of *all* the classes of creditors are best served by attempting to continue the business of the company.

(h) Recommendations as to the course which should be taken in relation to the company, including, if warranted, draft proposals for a compromise or a scheme of arrangement.
In the limited time available so far, an examiner is unlikely to have formulated detailed proposals for a compromise or scheme of arrangement, though if he has managed to draft proposals it is helpful to exhibit them. If he believes that the company and its business is capable of survival, he will usually express the view that the court protection should be continued in order to allow the preparation of proposals for a scheme of arrangement. Any negotiations with the creditors or potential investors can thus continue with this in mind.

(i) His opinion as to whether the facts disclosed would warrant further enquiries with a view to proceedings under section 297 or 297A of the Principal Act (inserted by the Companies Act 1990), or both.
This deals with the possibility that an officer of the company may have been guilty of fraudulent or reckless trading. In the short period of time available to him the examiner may be unable to come to a conclusive opinion on this matter. He can, however, express a view based on the information available to him to date as to whether further enquiries are warranted. If he has already conducted interviews with directors and other officers (or has been obstructed in his attempts to do so), he should of course say so.

(j) *Any other matters as the examiner thinks relevant or the court directs.*
This sub-section gives the examiner a wide discretion to include any other information of significance which he has not already dealt with. For example, he may wish to deal with specific matters such as the prospects for future employment, the nature and extent of discussions to date with potential investors, or other items he regards as important.

The court may also have given directions at the application for directions stage or at the hearing at the petition that certain matters be addressed by the examiner. Again, these directions will vary depending on the circumstances of the company seeking protection and the petition generally. But it it is now clear that the court will expect the examiner to deal with at least three additional matters in every case. Firstly, he should consider whether or not there were any material errors in the petition and/or grounding affidavit leading to his appointment. Secondly, if the petition and/or grounding affidavit have set out proposals for the company's survival which are not now being adopted, the examiner should set out the reasons for their non-adoption.[10] The court has also indicated that it is desirable that the examiner consider whether any evidence adduced at the hearing of the petition was misleading in any material respect — and indeed that he should re-enter the matter for further consideration even before preparing his section 15 report if this is the position.[11]

(k) *His opinion as to whether his work would be assisted by a direction of the court extending the role or membership of any creditors' committee referred to in section 21.*
While section 21 provides the examiner with the power to appoint a committee of creditors to assist with the performance of his functions, no specific role is set out in the legislation for such a committee. The membership of the committee is limited to not more than five members (including the holders of the three largest secured claims who are willing to serve). It is conceivable that an examiner may find the formation of such a committee of help to him, for example, in ascertaining the identity and value of various creditors, and he may wish to increase the size of that committee in certain circumstances.

The court may also direct that the examiner investigate other matters, or carry on certain discussions, and may impose upon him generally such other duties as it deems appropriate.[12]

10.   *Re Clare Textiles Ltd*, footnote 8 above.
11.   *Re Wogans (Drogheda) Ltd (No. 2)*, High Court (unreported) 7 May 1992 (Costello J.).
12.   Section 15(2).

Delivery of the Report

Once the report is prepared (either within the prescribed time or such other time as the court may have fixed), the examiner makes an *ex parte* application to court for leave to deliver it. This application is grounded upon a verifying affidavit which should indicate:[13]

(i) whether the petitioner has delivered the requisite notice of the petition to the Registrar of Companies within three days of its presentation (whether or not this delivery has actually occurred is obviously a matter outside the examiner's control),

(ii) whether the examiner has advertised his appointment (and the date thereof) in *Iris Oifigiúil* and two daily newspapers in accordance with the limits in section 12(2)(b). He is also expected to indicate whether he has similarly advertised any date fixed for the hearing of any matters arising out of the section 15 report to be prepared; since such a date will usually only be fixed after the report has been delivered, this provision seems illogical,

(iii) whether he has delivered a copy of the order appointing him to the Registrar of Companies within three days of his appointment.[14] This appears to be an impracticably short period within which to expect an order to be drawn up in most situations,

(iv) whether any portions of the report should be omitted from delivery. The examiner is obliged[15] to deliver a copy of his report to the company on the same day that he delivers it to the court. But if a written application is made by an interested party, he is obliged to supply a copy of the report to that interested party also. 'Interested party' is not defined in this section but would certainly extend to members and creditors of the company. Where such an application has been received, the examiner may suggest the omission of certain parts of the copy of the report to be supplied. While the court has a general discretion to direct the omission of any information contained in the report, it will be particularly persuaded to exercise its discretion if it can be shown that the survival of the company (or the whole or any part of its undertaking) would be prejudiced by the inclusion of such information.[16] However this discretion will be exercised sparingly by the court.

13.   Rule 40.
14.   Section 12(3).
15.   Section 15(3).
16.   Section 15(5).

The examiner is also obliged in the affidavit to draw the attention of the court to any aspects of the report which may be relevant to the exercise by the court of any other of its functions under the Act. Since the court is empowered to deal specifically with fraudulent and reckless trading, and also to wind up the company or make other orders in respect of the assets, any matter relating to such powers would appear to be particularly relevant in this context.

The court does not approve or disapprove of the contents of the report filed by the examiner; the report is simply formally received, liberty to deliver it having been given. It is clear that receiving the report does not mean that the court has 'sanctioned' the statements or proposed courses of action contained in it.[17]

As provided in section 18, if the examiner is of the view that the whole (or part) of the undertaking of the company is capable of survival as a going concern, and that an attempt to do this would be more advantageous to the members as a whole (and creditors as a whole) than a winding up, which would be facilitated by the formulation of proposals, he is obliged, having so reported to the court under section 15, to begin to formulate such proposals. But it may frequently happen that because of certain views expressed and matters referred to in his report, it is appropriate for the court to hold a hearing to consider such matters. The court has no general discretion to direct the holding of a hearing, but is obliged to hold one if, in the examiner's opinion[18] (expressed in his report):

> (a) the whole or any part of the undertaking of the company is not capable of survival as a going concern, or
> (b) the survival of the undertaking in whole or part would not be facilitated by the formulation, acceptance or confirmation of proposals for a compromise or scheme of arrangement, or
> (c) an attempt to continue the whole or part of the undertaking is unlikely to be more advantageous to the members as a whole and the creditors as a whole than a winding-up of the company, or
> (d) there is (i) evidence of a substantial disappearance of property not adequately accounted for, or (ii) evidence of other serious irregularities in relation to the company's affairs.

The requirement to hold a hearing thus arises if any *one* of the above

17. See *Re Clare Textiles Ltd* (footnote 8 above). The court cannot thus be said to 'approve' costs or expenses incurred during the period prior to the report.
18. Section 17(1).
19. Rule 15.

conclusions is expressed by the examiner in his section 15 report. The protection continues, but a hearing should be held as soon as practicable, and the court may give directions as to any parties which should be notified, advertisements and in respect of any other matters as it sees fit.[19]

Section 17(2) indicates that the examiner, the company, any interested party (i.e. members and creditors) and any person referred to in the report in connection with any substantial disappearance of property or other serious irregularities shall be entitled to appear and to be heard at the hearing.

The court can make any order it sees fit following the hearing.[20] This wide discretion thus means that the protection will not necessarily be ended after such a hearing. The court might decide to continue protection, but on terms (e.g. the resignation of persons referred to in connection with company irregularities). The examiner may be directed to continue *in situ* to formulate proposals or meetings may be summoned to consider any such proposals for a compromise or scheme of arrangement. The court can even order that meetings of the board of directors or of the company generally be held to consider any matters which the court may direct.

But if the examiner has concluded that the company cannot be saved, and no evidence to controvert this is adduced at the hearing, it is likely that the court will order the winding-up of the company. Such a winding-up order takes effect from the date of the making of the order not from the date of the petition unless the court otherwise directs.[21] Alternatively, the court can direct the sale of the whole or part of the undertaking and may impose terms or conditions as to how the proceeds of such sale are to be distributed.[22] This may be an attractive option if a receiver had been appointed before the petition for protection had been presented, since the receiver can now be allowed back into the company again to carry on with the receivership. If necessary, a receiver may be appointed. This is one way in which the secured creditor's right to realise assets (which had been in abeyance during court protection) to discharge the company's indebtedness to him can now be restored.

The examiner (or such other person as may be directed by the court, such as the liquidator or receiver) shall deliver an office copy of any order made under section 17 at the hearing to the Registrar of Companies. A formal record of the conclusion of protection and commencement of the winding-up of the company is thus maintained.[23]

20.   Section 17(3).
21.   Section 17(6).
22.   Section 17(4)(d).
23.   Section 17(5).

CHAPTER 6

Proposals and Meetings

The obligation on an examiner to formulate proposals for a compromise or scheme of arrangement only arises if he has formed certain views about the company's future viability.[1] He must be of the opinion:

> (a) that the whole (or any part) of the undertaking of the company is capable of survival as a going concern, *and*
>
> (b) that an attempt to continue the whole (or part) of the company's undertaking would be likely to be more advantageous to the members and creditors as a whole than a winding-up, *and*
>
> (c) such survival would be facilitated by the formulation, acceptance and confirmation of proposals for a compromise or scheme of arrangement.[2]

The concept of formulating proposals designed to secure the future of a company appears in some respects to be inspired by sections 201-203 of the Companies Act 1963. These provisions allow a company to enter into an arrangement with its members or creditors which, if such arrangement is sanctioned by the court, will be binding on any dissenting minority of members or creditors and will thus enable the company to continue trading. Such arrangements may involve wide-ranging alterations to the rights of existing shareholders, including the issue of new shares or the acquisitions of all existing shares by a new holding company. A company may also agree with creditors to defer the due payment of its debt, or grant new forms of security or collateral. But the procedure has rarely been availed of, a voluntary or creditor's winding-up usually being the preferred option. The new process established by the 1990 Act is also quite different in a number of material respects, and so the earlier case law is of only limited assistance.

The contents of the proposals are set out in section 22(1). Other matters may be included as may seem appropriate or as the court directs.[3] The following are the primary requirements:

1. Or if the court has directed him to carry out this function after a hearing under section 17.
2. Section 18(1).
3. Section 22(4).

(a) The specification of each class of members and creditors of the company.

There is no definition in the Act of what constitutes a class of members or creditors. It is likely that the courts will continue to use the meaning set out in the judgment of Bowen L.J. in *Re Sovereign Life Assurance v Dodd*[4] that membership of each class 'must be confined to those persons whose rights are not so dissimilar as to make it impossible for them to consult together with a view to their common interest'.[5] The division of members and creditors into various classes must not lead to confiscation of rights or injustice. However, it appears that the fact that there may be some distinguishing features between different members of one class who have otherwise a common interest is not necessarily fatal to the constitution of them as a class. So, in *Re Pye (Ireland) Ltd*[6] an unsecured creditor voting in favour of a scheme of arrangement under section 201 of the Companies Act 1963 was also the holder of 25 per cent of the shares in the company. The scheme of arrangement allowed for a deferment of some of the company's debts to enable the development of its assets. Clearly this 'creditor' also had an interest in the scheme in his capacity as a member. However, the Supreme Court held that his inclusion in the class of unsecured creditors did not render that class improperly constituted, since there was no proof that his inclusion had prejudiced others in the class. The inclusion of a creditor of this nature in such a class may not affect the outcome of the voting of that class where a qualified majority is required.[7] But the Act provides that a simple majority in number of members (and a simple majority in number representing a majority in value of creditors) in each class is all that is required for proposals to be deemed accepted by that class.[8] Since the result of the vote might well be determined by the inclusion in the class of even one creditor with 'extraneous' interests, a court is likely to scrutinise extremely closely the composition of the classes if any allegation of impropriety is made.[9]

A common nature of the interests of certain groups will be readily apparent. So, members will usually be divided into classes of ordinary and

4.   (1892) 2 QB 573.
5.   At 582.
6.   Supreme Court (unreported), 17th April, 1985 (*ex tempore*).
7.   As is required under section 201.
8.   Section 23(3) and (4).
9.   A stricter view of classification in the context of shareholders appears to be taken in
        Re Hellenic and General Trust Ltd [1976] 1 WLR 123. See also in *Re John Power &
        Son Ltd* [1934] IR 412. See generally Usher, 'Company Law in Ireland' (1986), pp.
        292-301.

preferential shareholders. Secured and unsecured creditors should form separate classes. It is increasingly common for leasing creditors to form a separate class; arguably, such a class should be extended to include hire-purchase creditors and even retention of title creditors[10] since their interests are based in part on their claim of ownership of or title to property at present in the possession of the company.

The concept of the 'preferential creditor' is not provided for in the Act. Nevertheless, since the success or failure of a proposed scheme of arrangement is of particular interest to creditors who would be preferential in a winding-up of the company (which is the most frequent result if a scheme is not approved), a practice has developed of constituting a separate class of these creditors.[11] It seems clear that the Revenue Commissioners have no entitlement to be treated as a separate category of creditor.[12]

In addition, because the examiner is not in a position to adjudicate on the validity or likely outcome of potential legal actions or other outstanding claims against the company, it is prudent for him to group these claims into a separate class where necessary.

(b) The specification of any class of members and creditors whose interests or claims will not be impaired by the proposals.

(c) The specification of any class of members and creditors whose interests or claims will be impaired by the proposals.

Proposals for a scheme of arrangement may leave some members and creditors completely unaffected, while significantly adjusting the rights of others to their detriment. Since the Act provides that the court cannot confirm a proposed scheme of arrangement unless at least one class of members and one class of creditors whose interests or claims would be impaired by the scheme have voted to approve it, the concept of what constitutes 'impairment' is crucial. It is defined in section 22(5) and (6). Broadly speaking, the party's position will be impaired if it is weakened or in some way rendered less valuable or favourable. A creditor's claim is impaired if he receives less in payment of his claim than the full amount due in respect of the claim at the date of the presentation of the petition. So a creditor who under the proposed scheme of arrangement will only receive

10. See section 11(8).
11. Usually consisting of e.g. the Revenue Commissioners and employees of the company.
12. See *Re Pye (Ireland) Ltd*, Supreme Court (unreported), 17 April 1985 (*ex tempore*) reversing Costello J. High Court (unreported), 12 November 1984.

20p in the pound is obviously impaired. But a creditor who is to be paid in full by instalments, rather than immediately, but without any interest payable under his contract with the company may also be impaired. In *Re Jetmara Teoranta*,[13] Costello J. held that a bank who was to be paid the full amount due to it by instalments and who would receive less in interest than the interest to which it was contractually entitled was 'impaired' within the meaning of the section. The conversion of a bank overdraft to a term loan may also constitute an impairment of the bank's position in certain circumstances since the interest rate chargeable on a term loan may be lower than that chargeable on an overdraft.

A member's interest is impaired if: (i) the nominal value of his shareholding is reduced, (ii) the amount of any fixed dividend to which he is entitled is reduced, (iii) he is deprived of all or any rights accruing to him by virtue of his shareholding, (iv) his percentage interest in the total share capital is reduced, and (v) he is deprived of his shareholding. So a proposed scheme of arrangement which requires shareholders to waive all dividends due, or which dilutes the power of existing shareholdings, for example, by the issuing of new shares, could be said to 'impair' the interests of a member. Undoubtedly the concept of impairment will be developed and refined in future decisions.

(d) The provision of equal treatment for each claim or interest of a particular class, unless the holder of a particular claim or interest agrees to less favourable treatment.

In order to comply with this requirement, all members of a particular class must receive equal treatment under the proposals. So, if it is proposed to pay the unsecured creditors 20p in the pound, this must apply to all unsecured creditors. 'Treatment' in this context amounts not just to the amount payable but also to the time and mode of payment. But a member of a particular class may consent to *less favourable* treatment. For example, the class of unsecured creditors may include the directors of the company, who have provided unsecured loans to the company. A proposal put to this class might indicate that all the unsecured creditors except the directors will receive 20p in the pound, but the directors will write off their debts and will therefore receive nothing. The directors would clearly be receiving less favourable treatment, but provided they agree to this there is nothing improper about the proposal. There is no stipulation as to when or how such consent should be given, though for practical purposes it should be dealt with at the meetings of the members and creditors.

13.   [1992] 1 IR 147.

(e) Provision for the implementation of the proposals.

Most schemes of arrangement will involve some form of deferred (or reduced) payment to at least some of the company's creditors. It is appropriate to set out the timetable under which those payments will be made. It is also common for additional monies to be invested into the company by way of purchasing existing shares or in return for the issue of additional shares. It may be part of a proposed scheme of arrangement that the company will sell part of its undertaking to a named purchaser and use the proceeds to develop or upgrade the remainder of its business. In most cases it is unnecessary for creditors to enter into a written agreement with the company that they will accept deferred or reduced payments; they can vote to accept or reject this at the creditors' meetings. But the court has made it clear on a number of occasions that where a proposal involves the investment of additional funds or the sale of certain assets, such commitments should be in the form of unconditional written agreements.[14]

Any agreement of this nature should also have been concluded before the meetings of members and creditors to consider the proposals, so that the agreement itself forms part of the scheme and can be placed before the members and creditors for their consideration. Investors will presumably be entitled to insert a clause into any such agreement making it a condition precedent to the agreement taking effect that the court confirms the scheme of arrangement at the subsequent court hearing under section 24. But agreements which are conditional on the investor obtaining the necessary finance to make the investment, or which require prior clearance from the Revenue Commissioners for the purposes of tax, are unlikely to be regarded as sufficiently conclusive.

(f) Changes in the management or direction of the company considered necessary or desirable by the examiner to facilitate the survival of the company (and the whole or any part of its undertaking) as a going concern.

Poor financial control is regularly cited as a significant factor contributing to a company's insolvency. The examiner may thus recommend that a new financial management team be introduced or that an improved method of financial control be implemented. Other managerial or boardroom changes may also be appropriate. It may also be necessary for the company to concentrate its attention on a particular aspect of its business or even to extend its operation into a new project in a different area. Any such changes as may be relevant should be outlined in the proposals by the examiner.

14.   See *Wogans (Drogheda) Ltd (No. 2)*, High Court (unreported), 7 May 1992 (Costello J.) at pages 14 and 18 of the judgment.

(g) Changes in the memorandum or articles of association of the company which the examiner considers should be made, whether as regards the management or direction of the company, or otherwise.

The appointment of new directors or the issuing of additional shares may require alterations to the memorandum or articles of association of the company. The objects clause may also need to be extended.

(h) Such other matters as the examiner deems appropriate.

This gives a general discretion to the examiner. He may wish to deal with the position of particular members or creditors, or to indicate how other liabilities (such as personal guarantees given by directors) will be affected. It is also helpful for him to give an outline of how it is anticipated the business of the company will survive if the scheme is implemented.

The proposals (as formulated by the examiner) may thus ideally be reduced to writing for presentation to the meetings of members and creditors. The written format of the proposals should consist of:

> (i) the requirements set out at (a) to (h) above;
>
> (ii) any written agreements relating to investment, sale or otherwise as may be relevant,
>
> (iii) any other matters the court may have directed to be included,
>
> (iv) a statement of the assets and liabilities (including contingent and prospective liabilities) of the company at the date of the formulation of the proposals,[15]
>
> (v) an estimate of the financial outcome for each class of members and creditors if the company were to be wound up.[16] This enables members and creditors to assess the relative merits and drawbacks of voting in favour of or against the scheme of arrangement.

Meetings

Once the examiner has formulated the proposals in question, he is obliged to convene and preside at meetings of the members and creditors[17] for

---

15. Required under section 22(2).
16. Required under section 22(3).
17. Section 18(2) obliges him to convene such meetings of members and creditors as he thinks proper, though rule 18 makes it clear that he should notify *every* member and creditor appearing in the company's books. Cf. *Re British and Commonwealth Holdings plc (No. 3)* [1992] BCLC 322.

consideration of the proposals. Rule 18 sets out the procedures for the convening and conduct of meetings. It is unsurprising (in view of the relatively short time period during which court protection will be granted to a company) that the length of notice required for these meetings is reduced to a minimum of three days.[18] Notice of the meetings must be sent by post to all persons appearing in the company's books to be creditors or members of the company not less than three days before the appointed date of the meeting. It is not necessary to send a complete copy of the proposals to each member and creditor with the notice of the meetings. All that is required is a statement explaining the effect of the compromise or arrangement. Every effort should be made to ensure that such a statement is clear and unambiguous and, where possible, sets out the main facts which will enable the notice parties to exercise their judgment on the proposed scheme. It has been held in other circumstances that that the court has a duty to scrutinise very carefully circulars relating to complicated schemes of arrangement.[19]

There should also be sent a statement setting out the material interests of the directors (whether as members, creditors or otherwise) and the effect on those interests of the compromise or arrangement insofar as their interests may be affected differently from similar interests of other persons. This is a repetition of a requirement under the notification procedure for meetings to consider compromises and schemes of arrangements under section 201,[20] and appears to be designed to keep members and creditors informed of any possible additional advantages which directors-as-creditors (or members) might obtain from a proposed scheme. Since the proposals must treat constituents of each class of members and creditors equally, it is unlikely that directors will obtain any such additional advantages in another capacity. An examiner could, however, use this procedure to inform members and creditors of the effect of the proposed scheme (if any) on personal guarantees given by directors for company debts. A similar explanation must be given in respect of trustees of any deed for securing the issue of debentures where a compromise or arrangement affects the rights of debenture-holders of a company. Directors and trustees for debenture-holders are obliged to give such information as may be necessary to the examiner for these purposes.

General and special proxy forms must be sent to all members and

18. Section 18(2). Cf. section 133 of the Companies Act 1963 (as amended) for the much longer period of notice for annual general meetings and extraordinary general meetings.
19. See *Re Dorman Long & Co Ltd* [1934] 1 Ch. 635 at 655.
20. Section 202(1)(a).

creditors with the notice of meeting. The forms are similar to those used under the winding-up rules.[21] Where proxies are used, they should be lodged with the examiner not later than 4 p.m. on the day prior to the meeting. A creditor or member may also appoint the examiner to act as his proxy.

It is conceivable that a postal strike or other unusual circumstance might necessitate that notice of the meetings be advertised. Prior court sanction would be required for such a departure from the standard procedure, and the advertisement should make clear that a copy of the statement explaining the effect of the compromise or arrangement proposed can be obtained from the examiner on request.[22] In any event, if a complete copy of the proposals is requested by a creditor or a member, an examiner should accede to this request unless it is unreasonably onerous or inconvenient for him to do so.

The examiner is entitled to fix the time and place for the meetings of the members and creditors; it is not necessary that they all be held at the same time or place. He is obliged to preside and chair the meetings, and to ensure that they are conducted in an orderly manner so that proper discussion of the proposals may take place. He can also adjourn the meetings (with the consent of the meetings) as he sees fit.

Aside from adjourning, meetings cannot act unless there are present or represented:

> (i) at a creditors' meeting, at least three creditors ruled by the examiner as being entitled to vote,
> (ii) at a meeting of members, at least two members.

If not quorate, the meetings shall be adjourned for not less than three and not more than 21 days.[23]

It is possible for members or creditors to suggest modification to the proposals at these meetings. Practical difficulties may be caused if a modification is only introduced at the meeting of the last class, the other classes of members and creditors having already voted on the original scheme. It is hard to see how an examiner can avoid having to re-convene meetings of the other classes if the proposed scheme is modified by the meeting of one class, unless it is clear that the position of the parties in the other classes is not prejudiced by the modification. Any suggested modification can only be accepted with the consent of the examiner.[24]

21. Order 74, rule 75.
22. Section 23(7) applying section 202(2)(6) of the Companies Act 1963, as modified.
23. Section 144 of the Companies Act 1963 validates resolutions passed at adjourned meetings — see section 23(6).
24. Section 23(2).

As already indicated, a simple majority in number among the members present or represented in each class of members is sufficient to ensure that the proposals are deemed to have been accepted by that class. A simple majority in number representing a majority in value of the creditors present or represented at the meeting is likewise sufficient for acceptance in each class of creditor. So a very large unsecured creditor who is outnumbered at the meeting of unsecured creditors may still be able to defeat other unsecured creditors if the value of his claim exceeds all of their claims.

The Act contains an interesting provision which enables State authorities to compromise debts owed to them under a proposed scheme of arrangement.[25] Many 'State authorities' (which now include the State itself, a Minister of the Government, a local authority[26] or the Revenue Commissioners) were unable to support schemes of arrangement under section 201 because they were not entitled to compromise monies payable under statute to them. In so far as this section specifically empowers such an authority to accept less than what is owed notwithstanding any other statutory provision, it must surely be interpreted as a strongly persuasive statutory invitation (if not exhortation) to the Revenue Commissioners and similar bodies to vote in favour of such schemes, where appropriate. As yet, there is little evidence that this invitation has been accepted by State institutions.

In conducting the voting at the various meetings, the examiner has power to allow or disallow the vote of a party claiming to be a creditor, but his decision in this respect may be subject to appeal to the court. The debts of some parties claiming to be creditors will often be disputed by the company. If in doubt, the examiner should allow the party to vote on a 'without prejudice' basis. That party's vote may subsequently be declared invalid if it is successfully objected to in court. Even if no formal objection is subsequently taken, the court can still give whatever weight it deems appropriate to the views of creditors whose debts are in dispute.[27]

The examiner is obliged to keep minutes of the proceedings of the meetings. In particular, he should note the proposals put before the meetings, any modifications adopted to those proposals, and the outcome of each of the meetings, since he will be required to set out details of these matters in his report to the court under section 18. He should also keep a list of all members and creditors who are present at every meeting.

25.   Section 25(5).
26.   'Local authority' was added by section 180(1)(h) of the Companies Act 1990, presumably to allow local authorities to compromise claims for rates and other local charges.
27.   See *Wogans (Drogheda) Ltd (No. 1)*, footnote 14 above.

CHAPTER 7

Second Report of the Examiner

The examiner is obliged to report to the court the proposals put to the meetings of the various members and creditors, and the outcome of those meetings. Again, the time given to the examiner to fulfil this task is somewhat limited. He must formulate the proposals, call meetings of the members and creditors, put the proposals before them, note the outcome of the voting, then prepare a report and furnish it to the court; all within 42 days of his appointment. The examiner's first 21 days in office may frequently be spent assessing the future viability of the company and attempting to gather as much information as possible for this purpose. While it is not part of his stated functions to negotiate with creditors or members with a view to ascertaining what type of proposals would be most likely to be accepted, in practice it is most frequently the examiner who carries out this task. His status as a court-appointed officer means his independence is unlikely to be questioned by any hitherto suspicious creditors, and his examination of the company's business should give the information necessary to explore the feasibility of any practical solution.

It is possible that the 42 day time limit can be extended by the court. Section 18(2) specifically allows the court to enlarge the time for the applying of the second report. Delays necessitating such an extension may be due to protracted negotiations, difficulties in formulating the proposals or even setbacks encountered in an attempt to call meetings, as well as numerous other circumstances. In *Re N.S. Distribution Ltd* [1] it was held that an extension of time to hold creditors meetings will be granted where the administrator had diligently pursued his duties and there were sensible prospects of bringing the matter before the creditors in an orderly way. Harman J. suggested that 'the court in general should be willing to entertain applications for an extension of time in such circumstances'.[2] In Ireland, however, because of the very short protection period provided in the Act[3] and the possibility that an extension of time might result in the examiner

1.   1990 [BCLC] 169.
2.   At 170.
3.   Court protection is not rigidly limited to three months under the UK Insolvency Act.

certifying additional incurred expenses which would prejudice the priority of other creditors, the court is likely to be more circumspect in granting such extensions. The rules[4] provide that any application for an extension should be made *ex parte* within the original time limit. Any party affected by the extension granted may then apply (on notice to the examiner) to have the order set aside. To obviate any such subsequent application, the examiner should ground his application for an extension on time on affidavit. The affidavit should set out: (i) the progress in formulating the proposals and calling meetings to date as well as the reasons for delay, (ii) the estimate of additional time required, (iii) the likelihood of prejudice to any party that such an extension would create, and (iv) whether other additional certified expenses (if any) during such an extension would affect the priority or position of creditors.

An extension of the protection period in addition to the 42 days provided is also possible. But here again the three month time period set out in section 5(1) is likely to be quite strictly adhered to by the court, because of the limitations imposed on creditors in enforcing debts during the protection period as well as the alteration of the priority of debt which may be caused by the incurring of certified expenses. If an examiner (on an *ex parte* application, presumably) satisfies the court that he would be unable to report within the three month period set out in section 5(1) but will be able to report if the period of protection is extended, the court may extend the period by not more than 30 days to allow him to do so.[5] It seems likely that any party affected by such an extension could similarly apply to the court to set aside the extension order in a manner akin to that set out in rule 16.

In either case, unless the examiner can show he will be able to report to the court in the extended period, any such extension appears pointless.

Contents of the Report

Section 19 sets out the various matters which the second report of the examiner must contain.

(a) The proposals placed before the required meetings.

Details of the matters to be dealt with have already been set out in chapter 6. The report should give a summary of this information, as well as the financial details of how these proposals will affect the various classes of members and creditors.

4.   Rule 16.
5.   Section 18(3).

(b) Any modification of those proposals adopted at any of those meetings.

The examiner should ensure that any such modification adopted was properly accepted and voted upon by the relevant classes. Details of how this occurred may be set out in this part of the report.

(c) The outcome of each of the required meetings.

The procedure to be adopted for voting at these meetings has already been outlined. In addition, in setting out the result of the vote of each class of members and creditors, the examiner can also set out here: (i) whether the proposals constitute the impairment of any class's claim or interests under section 22(5) and (6), and (ii) whether each class has accepted or rejected the proposals in accordance with the provisions of section 23(3) and (4).

(d) The recommendation of the committee of creditors (if any).

The examiner is obliged to provide any committee of creditors appointed by him with a copy of the proposals.[6] The committee may then express an opinion or recommendation on the proposals. It is likely that any such opinion or recommendation would be taken into consideration by the court in deciding whether or not to confirm the proposals, hence its inclusion in the report.

(e) A statement of the assets and liabilities (including contingent and prospective liabilities) of the company as of the date of the report.

This is essentially an update for the court of the financial position as originally set out in the examiner's report under section 15. It is appropriate to include in the report:

> (i) the amount of certified expenses incurred during the protection period and,
> (ii) the estimated cost of the fees and expenses of the examiner,

since these items will both be treated as liabilities of the company.

(f) A list of the creditors of the company.

The creditors should be listed in accordance with the manner that they were classified for the purposes of the meeting. Even disputed creditors can thus

6.   Section 21(3).

be listed. In addition to listing and classifying the creditors, the report should show:

> (i) the amount owing to each creditor,
> (ii) the nature and value of any security held by any secured creditor,
> (iii) the priority status of any secured creditor under section 285 of the Companies Act 1963 or any other statutory provision or rule of law.

The last requirement refers to the preferential status in a winding-up accorded to certain debts under section 285[7] of the Companies Act 1963 (such as certain wages and statutory remuneration due to employees, local rates, and outstanding PAYE, PRSI, VAT and other taxes) as well as under other legislation.[8]

It is conceivable that creditors who have such preferential status in a winding-up will have less weight attached by the court to any opposition expressed by them to the scheme of arrangement, being somewhat more 'protected' if the scheme is not confirmed and the company goes into liquidation. Frequently, however, even preferential creditors are not paid in full in a winding-up, and so the 'protected' status of such creditors may be more apparent than real.

(g) A list of officers of the company.

This will almost certainly be a repetition of the matters already referred to in the equivalent part of the first report under section 15, unless new information indicates the existence of additional officers.

(h) The recommendations of the examiner.

The views of the examiner will be of considerable interest to the court. He is an independent court-appointed officer, and can thus express dispassionately his opinion as to whether or not the scheme of arrangement proposed would, if confirmed, secure the future viability of the company. For example, if the meetings of the members and creditors to consider the proposed scheme of arrangement have been inconclusive, or have not resulted in some sort of general (though not necessarily unanimous)

---

7.   As amended by section 10 of the Companies (Amendment) Act 1982.
8.   For example, the 'super-preferential' status given to certain payments due to employees under the Social Welfare (Consolidation) Act 1981. See also the Protection of Employees (Employer's Insolvency) Act 1984.

agreement, he may feel that there is no practical alternative to liquidation. In setting out his conclusions on these matters, the examiner should endeavour to indicate clearly the reasoning behind his opinion. In certain circumstances he may recommend modifications which may have become necessary since the meetings where held; the court can then confirm the proposals subject to modification[9] as it sees fit. It may also be appropriate to make other recommendations relating to the timetable of the imple- mentation of the scheme, or in respect of such other matters as he sees fit.

(i) Such other matters as the examiner deems appropriate or as the court directs.

Additional information which may assist the court in deciding whether to confirm the proposed scheme of arrangements should prudently be included by the examiner. Such material will vary in accordance with the circum- stances of each individual examinership. Of particular relevance in nearly all cases, however, is a comparative analysis of the estimated financial outcome for each class of members and creditors:

(i) in the event of the scheme being confirmed,

(ii) in the event of the company being wound up (or in the event of a receiver being appointed to the company if the company is threatened by receivership). This will allow the court to assess the effect of the con- firmation or non-confirmation on the various classes, as well as helping it to decide what weight to attach to the views expressed by those classes.

The examiner must also ensure the agreements relating to the future investment in the company are appended (in binding written form) to this report. The court may also direct that certain specified matters be addressed in the examiner's second report. The outcome of any investigation or enquiry held by him into possible fraudulent or reckless trading by the company is an example of the type of information which the court may require to be included.

Rule 17(2) requires that the report contain a full account of each meeting convened by the examiner and of the proposals put before those meetings, as well as an appendix of the proposals dealing with each of the matters specified in section 22 in the order.

---

9.   Section 24(3).

Delivery of the Report

The examiner effects delivery of the report by making an *ex parte* application to the court to deliver it.[10] He is obliged also on the same day to deliver a copy of the report (a) to the company and (b) to any interested party who applies in writing,[11] but he can request in his *ex parte* application to the court that certain portions of the report be omitted before being delivered to any such interested party and the court may direct the omission of such portions accordingly.[12] A possible example is where a new investor into a company does not wish his identity to be revealed publicly (as distinct from to the court) unless and until the scheme of arrangement has been approved.

The court simply receives the report; it does not approve it or its contents in any way. The court will usually fix a date for the hearing, and may make directions in respect of notification to parties of the hearing date as it sees fit. Because of the short time periods involved, it is quite possible that the report may be delivered within the three months period (as extended by an additional 30 days where appropriate under section 18(3)) but that the hearing date and consequent determination of whether or not the proposed scheme of arrangement should be confirmed fall outside this time limit. Section 18 (4) provides specifically for this eventuality. The court is empowered to extend the time necessary for it to take a decision under section 24 (on whether or not to confirm the proposals) once the report has been filed within the time limit. Such an extension may be granted as a result of an application by the examiner[13] (in which circumstances the court may direct that notice of any such application for an extension be served on other parties as it sees fit), or the court may simply extend the time of its own motion. In this way the company can continue under the protection of the court until the hearing is concluded and a decision is made on whether or not the proposed scheme should be confirmed (including, possibly, time required for the determination of any appeal).

If the examiner reports that it is not possible to reach an agreement on a compromise or scheme of arrangement at the meetings, the court has a number of options. It may simply withdraw court protection immediately and make no further orders. Alternatively, it may make an order for the winding-up of the company.[14] While the proceeding to be adopted is unclear, it would seem sensible to adopt rule 20 so that when the examiner reports on this matter to the court, the court may order the examiner or any other person to apply forthwith to have the company wound up.

10. Rule 17(1).
11. Section 18(5).   12. Section 18(6).
13. Rule (3).   14. Section 14(11)(b).

CHAPTER 8

Hearing of the Proposals

One of the fundamental differences between the Insolvency Act in the United Kingdom and the Irish Act is the requirement here that any proposed compromise or scheme of arrangement be sanctioned by the court before becoming effective. Majorities in value of the meetings of members and creditors are sufficient to implement an administrator's proposals under the Insolvency Act[1] without the necessity for court approval. As already indicated,[2] that legislation gives a veto to a secured creditor who has appointed a receiver which may prevent the whole process of administration. In addition, since an administration order is made only where the court is satisfied that it is likely that one or more of the purposes specified by the Insolvency Act will be achieved,[3] it is arguable that any scheme put forward by an administrator should attempt to achieve the specific purpose for which the order was originally made.

The Irish Act contains none of these limitations. The court is entrusted to ensure that any scheme proposed is fair, equitable and not unfairly prejudicial to any interested party. While the jurisdiction given to the court in this respect appears wide, certain preconditions must be fulfilled before this jurisdiction can be exercised.

Parties

Section 24(2) provides that the following parties may appear and be heard at the hearing to consider the examiner's second report:

> (a) the company,
> (b) the examiner, and
> (c) any creditor or member whose claim or interest would be impaired if the proposals were implemented.

1. See section 23 thereof. Approval of schemes of arrangement under section 201 of the 1963 Act require qualified majorities in favour of 75 per cent of each class meeting, but these are not required under the 1990 Act.
2. See Chapter 2 above.
3. See section 8(1) thereof.

There is thus no statutory entitlement given to, for example, unimpaired members or creditors to appear or be heard. But the word 'may' contained in this section is likely to be interpreted as being permissive. The court has a general discretion to hear other persons *de bene esse*, and is unlikely to shut out such parties who wish to address the court or whose view may be of assistance, though the court can attach whatever weight it sees fit to any such submissions. So, for example, a single large creditor (e.g. a bank) whose claim is unimpaired by the proposed scheme may still be permitted to address the court and may be of assistance in showing how the future of the company will be provided for. The exercise of this discretion by the court will depend on the circumstances of each case, but it may be that even a party who has no previous relationship with the company will be heard. So, in *Re 3V Multimedia Group*[4] the court allowed a proposed investor to address the court on the extent of a modification which the court had made to a proposed scheme.

Procedure

There is no set procedure for the hearing. Affidavits in support or in opposition should be exchanged between the parties prior to the hearing, though there is no requirement that notice be given of intention to appear. Usually the examiner will begin the hearing by presenting his report, opening any affidavits and expressing his views on the proposed scheme. Opponents and proponents of the scheme may then be heard in whatever order the court sees fit, as well as any other parties which the court in its discretion decides to allow. It is appropriate now to consider the various grounds of opposition on which opponents of the scheme may rely.

Grounds of Opposition

While the specific grounds of objection are set out in section 25, a variety of criteria are also set out in section 24, which criteria must be met before the court can exercise its discretion to confirm a scheme. Thus, an opponent of a scheme who can establish that one of the criteria under section 24 has not been met will be in a position to oppose the scheme. The undoubtedly wide discretion granted to the court is clearly subject to the provisions of section 24 and section 25, so if grounds of objection are successfully established under either or both of these sections, the scheme cannot be confirmed.

4.   High Court (unreported), 20 August 1992 (*ex tempore*) (Costello J.).

Some of the grounds of objection may be classified as procedural (rather than substantive) in nature. For example, an impaired member or creditor may object that there was some material irregularity at or in relation to a meeting at which the proposals were put forward for the consideration of members and creditors under section 23.[5]

The key word here is 'material'. A failure to comply with some of the procedures set out in the rules will not automatically render the meetings void[6] unless specifically so directed by the court. But a failure to classify the various types of members and creditors or to provide for proper voting might be regarded as a 'material' irregularity if it is shown that the outcome of the meetings was affected in an important or relevant manner. So the failure to include a small opposing unsecured creditor in the voting of his class where the rest of that class unanimously voted to support the scheme might not be seen as 'material' since his vote could not have affected the decision of the class to approve the scheme. But where the vote is extremely tight, the incorrect classification or exclusion of even one creditor might affect the outcome and could even mean the difference between acceptance or rejection of the scheme by that class. Such an irregularity is likely to be regarded as 'material'.

Material irregularity is not confined to the *conduct* of the meetings. An objector could allege that the *proposals* put before the meetings did not provide for equal treatment for each claim or interest within a particular class, or were in some other way in breach of the requirements of section 22(1). Since the contents of the proposals put forward are undoubtedly matters 'relating to' the meetings, such an irregularity might again be deemed to be material, particularly if it also amounts to a breach of section 22(1).[7] In general what is material will depend on the effect of the irregularity in question as well as the circumstances of each case.

An impaired objector might also argue that acceptance of the proposals by the meeting (or, presumably, meetings) was obtained by improper means.[8] What this will mean will depend on the circumstances of each individual case; an example might be where a side-agreement was entered into between the company and certain creditors which promised additional benefits outside of the proposals in order to procure the votes of those creditors at the meetings. So even where no irregularity occurred at or in

---

5.   Section 25 (1)(a).
6.   Order 124, rule 1 of the rules of the Superior Court.
7.   In *Re Carrybox Shipping Ltd*, High Court (unreported), 21 August 1991 (*ex tempore*) (Carroll J.) an objection on this basis was upheld. New meetings were ordered by the court under section 25(3).
8.   Section 25(1)(b).

relation to the meeting, an impaired member or creditor could still object to the methods used to gain acceptance for the proposals. Although no case-law exists on the point, some form of improper or misleading conduct (e.g. where an examiner in putting proposals before a meeting misled those at the meeting as to the true effect of the proposals) would probably be required before such an objection would be upheld. Significantly, even a person who voted in favour of the proposals at the meetings can object to confirmation by the court on this ground.[9]

An objector may also argue that the proposals put before the meetings were put forward for an improper purpose.[10] Again, a person who voted in favour of the proposals and then became aware that they had been put forward for an improper purpose may still object to their confirmation at the court hearing. What constitutes an improper purpose is extremely difficult to define. In stating that a court *cannot* confirm a scheme the sole or primary purpose of which is the avoidance of payment of tax due,[11] the Act clearly indicates that avoidance of tax due is an 'improper' purpose, at least if that is the sole or primary purpose. But many schemes will involve the payment of a dividend of less than the full amount owing to the Revenue Commissioners along with other unsecured creditors. While this clearly amounts to non-payment of some part of the total amount of tax due, it is not necessarily improper. Indeed, given the requirement that creditors should be treated equally within each class, to 'prefer' the Revenue Commissioners by paying the full amount claimed above other creditors in the same class could itself be improper.[12]

Aside from avoidance of tax due, a court may in its discretion accept submissions that the proposed scheme would, if confirmed, achieve a certain purpose which is improper in the circumstances. A common example is a scheme which purports to release the directors from personal guarantees given by them for the company's debts. There may be no justification for releasing the directors from such guarantees, particularly, for example, where a bank who may only receive a fraction of the debt owed to it would now also have to forego any right of action against the guarantors/directors. In *Re Selukwe Ltd*,[13] Costello J. accepted such an argument from a bank which would only obtain 10 per cent of its total debt under a proposed scheme. Holding that the proposals were not fair and equitable to the bank, Costello J. modified the proposals by deleting the

9. Section 25 (2)(a).
10. Section 25 (1)(c).
11. Section 24(4)(b).
12. Unless the other creditors consent to this course.
13. High Court (unreported), 20 December 1991.

paragraph relating to the release of the guarantees and inserting instead a clause indicating that nothing in the scheme would affect the liability of the directors on foot of their personal guarantees to the banks. This seemed a sensible solution; the proposed scheme was in many other respects satisfactory.

Indeed, the effect of a scheme of arrangement on personal guarantees is clearly a relevant matter for the court to take into consideration. Despite the suggestion that such guarantees are automatically discharged by confirmation of a scheme,[14] the better view is that the scheme should specifically provide for how the guarantees are to be dealt with. It may be that it is appropriate to release certain directors (e.g. those who are waiving loans to the company or making some other financial contribution) from their guarantees, or perhaps to provide that the guarantees will lapse if the company pays all sums falling due under the scheme.[15] But it is clear that if these guarantees are not discharged, contingent liabilities continue to exist against the company in favour of the guarantors who have rights in subrogation. The scheme should thus specifically deal with how these subrogation rights are to be limited, otherwise the future of the scheme and the company may be jeopardised by such a guarantor's claim.[16]

It is conceivable that other objectives of a scheme could be considered improper; for example, the avoidance of payment of *future* tax, or the establishment of a new commercial enterprise to the detriment of creditors and employees of the old enterprise.[17] Ultimately, what constitutes an 'improper' purpose is a matter for the court in the circumstances of each case. Arguably, an examiner may not have been motivated by any improper purpose in putting forward proposals for a scheme of arrangement, but the court's discretion appears to allow it refuse to confirm proposals which have improper consequences.

Before a court can confirm any proposals, it must be satisfied of certain principal matters.

(a) *At least one class of members and one class of creditors whose interests or claims would be impaired by the implementation of the proposals must have voted to accept the proposals.*[18]

14.   Section 24(6).
15.   See *Re Preswell Ltd*, High Court (unreported), 7 November 1991 (*ex tempore*) (Murphy J.).
16.   *Re Wogans (Drogheda) Ltd (No. 2)*, High Court (unreported), 7 May 1992 (Costello J.).
17.   See *Re Wogan's (Drogheda) Ltd (No. 2)*, footnote 16 above.
18.   Section 24(4)(a).

The voting procedures and the concept of 'impairment' have already been dealt with in chapter 6.

(b) *The avoidance of payment of tax due must not be the sole purpose, or a primary purpose, of the proposals.*[19]

This has already been dealt with above. The extent to which the payment of only part of a debt owed to the Revenue Commissioners is a *purpose* or a side-effect of a scheme, and whether, if a purpose, it is the *sole* or *primary* purpose, is a matter for the court.

(c) *The proposals must be fair and equitable in relation to any class of members or creditors that has not accepted the proposals, whose interests or claims would be impaired by implementation.*[20]

To consider this matter, the court takes an overview of the effect of the proposed scheme on the various classes of members and creditors. The court may examine whether the scheme operates fairly as between the various different classes, although the fact that some classes may not have their interests or claims impaired does not of itself make the scheme unfair or inequitable. Confirmation of the proposed scheme of arrangement by the court is not simply a 'rubber-stamping' of the votes of the class meetings. While the case-law relating to sanctions of schemes under sections 201-204 of the 1963 Act is of limited assistance, it does show that the court regards itself as having a power to test objectively the fairness of a scheme before giving sanction.[21] The principle stated by Bowen L.J. in *Re Alabama, New Orleans, Texas and Pacific Junction Railway Company*[22] is hard to argue with. He said[23]

> '. . . a compromise or arrangement which has to be sanctioned by the court must be reasonable, and no arrangement or compromise can be said to be reasonable in which you can get nothing and give up everything. A reasonable compromise must be a compromise which can, by reasonable people conversant with the subject, be regarded as beneficial to those on both sides who are making it. Now, I have no doubt at all that it would be improper for the court to allow an arrangement to be forced on any class . . . , if the arrangement cannot reasonably be supposed by sensible business people to be for the benefit for that class as such . . . .'

19. Section 24(4)(b).   20. Section 24 (4)(c)(i).
21. *Re John Power & Son Ltd* [1934] IR 412.
22. [1891] 1 Ch. 213.   23. At 243.

Obviously the Act expressly provides for the 'forcing' of a scheme of arrangement on a class who voted against it as the court sees fit. A scheme which impairs the position of a creditor may appear to be of little benefit in absolute terms, but compared to the likely outcome for such a creditor in a liquidation or a receivership, the dividend he receives under a scheme of arrangement may be significantly more substantial. The court have continued to consider proposed schemes from the objective viewpoint of the 'sensible business person'. For example, the proportion of the company's debt borne by a particular impaired class of objectors may be evidence of an inequitable or unreasonable scheme. Naturally, a court will have considerable regard for the views of the examiner as to whether or not the scheme is fair and equitable in its treatment of the various classes.

(d) *The proposals must not be unfairly prejudicial to the interests of any interested party.*[24]

This is also a ground upon which an objector is specifically entitled to rely under section 25(1). Clearly, many if not most schemes of arrangement will involve some degree of impairment (and therefore prejudice) to the claims or interests of some parties. The real issue is whether the extent of the prejudice suffered could be such as to be deemed 'unfair'. One approach is to compare the treatment which one creditor is receiving with the treatment of other creditors *in the same class*. This would require an unsecured creditor, for example, to show that he was being treated unfairly *qua* an unsecured creditor, possibly because other unsecured creditors in the class were receiving a bigger dividend or being paid more quickly. This approach has received some support in England, where a petition by a member to prevent a company undertaking a new line of business on grounds of, *inter alia*, 'unfair prejudice' to his interests failed on the grounds that the petitioner had not shown that his interests *as a member* had been dealt with any differently to the same interests of other members.[25] Since the proposals themselves are supposed to provide equal treatment for each claim or interest within a class,[26] such a scheme would be unlikely to be confirmed anyway. But this seems too narrow a definition of the concept; a number of English decisions have interpreted 'unfair prejudice' by looking beyond the specific class interests of affected persons and having regard to wider

24.   Section 24(4)(c)(ii).
25.   *Re a company* [1983] BCLC 126. The petition was brought under section 75 of the UK Companies Act 1980.
26.   Section 26(1)(d).

equitable considerations.[27] It is likely, too, that the court will apply an objective rather than subjective test of whether an interested party's interests have been unfairly prejudiced;[28] it should not be necessary for an interested party to show that the proposals were put forward by the examiner and accepted by other parties in a deliberate or conscious attempt to interfere unfairly with that person's interests.

Is a creditor who would do better in a winding-up or receivership unfairly prejudiced by a proposed scheme of arrangement? This argument has been used by the Revenue Commissioners on a number of occasions in opposing the confirmation of proposals. Since they are usually the largest preferential creditor, it is quite possible that if the company were wound up they would be paid in full, leaving nothing for the unsecured creditor. Yet the Act does not provide for the giving of 'preference' to any class of creditors although examiners will often hold a separate meeting for creditors who would be preferential in a winding-up and they may often be treated differently under a scheme than other creditors. It is arguable that the failure of the legislature to provide specially for preferential creditors in the Act was a deliberate attempt to move away from the priorities of debt which exist in a winding-up. The inference is that even if a scheme is not as favourable as a winding-up might be for certain creditors, the overall fairness of the scheme to the interests of *all* interested parties may justify it being confirmed by the court. So schemes have been sanctioned in which only a fraction of the preferential debt owing would be paid[29] and where payment of the preferential debt would be paid only over a period of six years.[30]

A similar stance has often been taken by the secured creditors of companies. Such a creditor's claim may be impaired even if the full amount due is being paid under the proposed scheme, perhaps because of delays in payment with no provision for interest, as previously indicated.[31] An even more dramatic prejudice suffered by a secured creditor is the restriction or

27. English courts have considered the meaning of 'unfair prejudice' in the context of a petition to re-order a company's affairs under section 459 of the Companies Act 1985 on a number of occasions; *Re A company* [1985] BCLC 18; *Re R.A. Noble & Sons (Clothing) Ltd* [1983] BCLC 273; *Re A company* [1986] BCLC 379; *Re Posgate and Denby (Agencies) Ltd* [1987] BCLC 8.

28. See *R.A. Noble & Sons (Clothing) Ltd* [1983] BCLC 273 (following *Re Bovey Hotel Ventures Ltd*).

29. *Re Selukwe Ltd*, footnote 13 above.

30. *Re Gallaghers Boxty House Ltd*, High Court (unreported), 5 November 1991 (*ex tempore*) (Denham J.). Revenue 'priority' debts may be repaid over a period of six years under the Chapter 11 procedure of the United States.

31. *Re Jetmara Teoranta*, High Court (unreported), 10 May 1991 (Costelloe J.).

removal of his right to sell the company property charged to him, which would be a course open to him under most debentures in a receivership. In so far as it amounts to a limitation on a secured creditor's right to exercise a validly obtained interest in the company property, this is surely an interference with the right to transfer property guaranteed by Article 43 of the Constitution. Such a right may, of course, be waived,[32] but in the absence of a clear waiver, such a restriction may be regarded as an unjust attack on the property rights of the secured creditor, particularly if there is no compensation for this restriction.[33] 'Compensation' in this context could mean (a) the amount due and owing, (b) the value of the interest in the property if sold as a going concern, or (c) the value of the interest in the property on a break-up basis. A secured creditor who simply wishes to exercise his charge over specific company property without necessarily selling on *the business* of the company can hardly argue for payment of a sum equivalent to the 'going concern' valuation. However, the 'break-up' valuation of the property may be considerably less than the amount due. Undoubtedly, the treatment of secured creditors is one of the most worrying aspects of the legislation. It can, of course, be argued that as the Constitution permits the limitation of the exercise of property rights in accordance with principles of social justice and the exigencies of the common good, this legislation is unimpeachable, since it attempts to provide a mechanism to allow ailing companies (and their employees) to survive, where appropriate. It may be suggested that the survival as a going concern of companies and jobs which might otherwise be lost is in the interests of the common good. In so far as the philosophy of the Act does not appear to countenance that the fate of the company and those who depend on it should lie solely in the hands of the large 'protected' creditors,[34] it may also be argued the legislation allows for re-adjustment of the imbalance between different types of creditors in the interests of social justice. But it is unlikely that this aspect of the legislation will escape constitutional scrutiny for long.

An interested party may also object to the proposed scheme on the basis that it deprives such a party of his right of action against the directors or other personnel involved in the running of the company.

As already indicated, one interpretation of section 24(6) would mean that confirmation of a proposed scheme confines creditors to enforcing whatever rights they may have obtained under *the scheme*, but does not necessarily allow them to pursue pre-existing alternative courses of action

32.   See e.g. *G. v An Bord Uchtála* 113 ILTR 25.
33.   *Central Dublin Development Association v Attorney General* 109 ILTR 69.
34.   See particularly the judgment of McCarthy J. in *Atlantic Magnetics*, Supreme Court (unreported), 5 December 1991.

(e.g. by suing directors on foot of personal guarantees). This interpretation of the section is not conclusive;[35] the wording of the section is tortuous and somewhat unclear, and it is of course possible to modify a scheme so as to allow creditors to retain their rights of action on such guarantees.[36] But a member or creditor may also wish to pursue members of the management for fraudulent or reckless trading. This appears only to be possible during the period of court protection (or in the course of a winding-up).[37] It is almost inconceivable that such proceedings would be commenced and concluded within the normal time limits under the Act, and since court protection ceases not more than 21 days after the confirmation of a proposed scheme, a creditor wishing to pursue such a remedy faces considerable difficulties unless either the time limit is artificially extended (with possible resulting prejudice to other creditors) or the company is wound up.[38]

This is 'unfair prejudice' in a very wide sense; effectively the objector is saying that to allow the management to escape their personal liabilities (actual or potential) is too high a price to pay for the survival of the company.

To some extent the court (or the scheme itself) may attempt to allay concerns of objectors in this respect by making it a condition that certain directors resign their positions and take no further part in the company. In other situations where the management of the company have inexplicably and persistently failed to make tax returns, the court has suspended a 'sword of Damocles' over the company by making it a condition of the scheme that if at any time during the operation of the scheme the company should fail to pay its current taxes as they fall due, the full amount of the Revenue Commissioners' debt would be immediately reactivated as being due and owing, and the Revenue Commissioners would be entitled to re-enter the proceedings to have the company wound up. While perhaps unappealing to potential investors, it does at least place the onus on them to appoint responsible management where necessary.

(e) *The company (and all or some of its undertaking) must be capable of survival as a going concern, survival being facilitated by the scheme and being likely to be more advantageous to the members as a whole and creditors as a whole than a winding-up of the company.*

---

35. In *Wogans (Drogheda) Ltd (No. 2)* (footnote 16 above) Costello J. appeared to regard the question as to whether or not certain guarantees were extinguished by the scheme of arrangement as open.
36. As was done in *Re Selukwe*, footnote 16 above.
37. See section 297A of the 1963 Act as amended by the Companies Act 1990.
38. For a good analysis of these difficulties, see Murphy J.'s judgment in *Dublin Heating Company v Hefferon and Others* [1992] ILRM 51.

While these are not stated in section 24 or section 25 as express requirements,[39] it is inconceivable that a court would confirm a proposed scheme where a company was *not* capable of survival in this way. *Prima facie* evidence of the future viability of the company in this regard will usually be provided in the examiner's report. One of the matters which it may be prudent for an examiner and the court to consider is whether there are any adverse tax consequences arising out of the successful implementation of a scheme. For example, the company may be liable for additional tax on debts which have been released (wholly or partly) under section 24(1) of the Finance Act 1980, where previously deductions may have been allowed for these debts.[40] Difficulties may also arise as a result of the reduction of VAT refunds since the amounts being paid to creditors may be significantly reduced as a result of the scheme. It is unlikely that any special dispensation will be given by the Revenue Commissioners to companies in this position unless specifically authorised by new legislation to do so, despite its power to compromise claims under section 23(5). Such companies will thus continue to be treated in accordance with the normal legal principles of taxation.[41]

The court is given power to confirm, confirm subject to modification or refuse to confirm the proposals as *it thinks proper*.[42] This appears to be an absolute discretion, and while it must be exercised judicially, the court is clearly entitled to take into account any other considerations which may be relevant to the circumstances of each individual case.[43] In imposing modifications, the court does not have to summon new meetings of the members and creditors to consider them unless the modifications were such as to fundamentally alter the proposed scheme.[44]

It is possible that some (or indeed all) of the proposals of the examiner will not impair the interests of any member or creditor. The court is empowered to confirm a scheme containing such proposals notwithstanding the requirements set out in section 24(4).[45]

---

39.   See *Clare Textiles (in liquidation)* [1993] 2 IR 213.
40.   Whether court approval of the proposed scheme constitutes a 'release' for tax purposes has not yet been decided.
41.   See *Wogans (Drogheda) Ltd (No. 2)*, footnote 16 above.
42.   Section 24(3).
43.   See *Re Goodman International*, High Court (unreported), 28 January 1991 (Hamilton P.).
44.   See *Re Goodman International*, footnote 43 above.
45.   Section 24(12).

Effect of Confirmation of Proposals

The court may take time after the hearing to make its decision. The protection period can be extended during this period by the court (of its own motion or on the application of the examiner) as is necessary.[46] But even if it decides to confirm the proposals, the scheme does not automatically come into effect. The court will fix a date, not later than 21 days from the date of its confirmation, for the proposed scheme of arrangement to come into effect.[47] Other orders for the implementation of its decision may also be made as the court sees fit. Such orders might, for example, relate to modifications introduced by the court. Changes to the memorandum and articles of association of the company set out in the proposals also take effect from the date fixed by the court. A copy of the order made by the court should be delivered by the examiner (or such other person as the court directs) to the Registrar of Companies, notice of which should be published in *Iris Oifigiúil*.

Once the proposals are confirmed, they are binding on all members and creditors affected by the proposals, as well as the company itself.[48] The adjustment of members' interests may be reflected in the memorandum and articles of association. Considerable attention has been given to the effect of confirmation on the rights of creditors. Whatever about the effect on a creditor's rights to pursue 'parallel' reliefs (such as personal guarantees given by directors), it is clear that other reliefs such as claims of fraudulent or reckless trading cannot be pursued once the protection period ends, which occurs on the date the scheme comes into effect[49] (unless the company is wound up). It also appears that creditors will now be confined to pursuing only claims provided for under the scheme; a creditor who is to receive 10p in the pound can only seek this amount, the balance no longer being a claim against the company. Creditors seeking to repossess goods under the leasing agreements or retention of title clauses will similarly be confined to the dividend and terms prescribed in the scheme. Nor can the creditor claim the balance against any other person who is liable 'under any statute, enactment, rule of law or otherwise' for all or any of the debts of the company.[50]

This would certainly seem *prima facie* to release guarantors and other parties to whom the company may have assigned its debts, though the terms of the scheme may leave this issue open.

Once a scheme comes into effect, the protection of the court ceases and

46.   Section 18(4).
47.   Section 24(9).
48.   Section 24(5) and (6).
49.   Section 26(1)(a).
50.   Section 24(6).

the appointment of the examiner terminates.[51] There is no procedure for re-entering the proceedings to monitor the progress of the scheme or otherwise, though there seems no reason why this could not be done, albeit without the protection of the court. It is, however, possible for the company or any interested party to apply to have the confirmation of proposals revoked if the confirmation was procured by fraud.[52] Such an application must be made within 180 days of the confirmation of the proposals. Initially it is an *ex parte* application to court for directions granted on an affidavit which should give full particulars of the fraud alleged. Since the court may revoke the confirmation on such terms it thinks fit, particular attention must be paid to parties who have already acquired interests or property in good faith and for value in reliance on that confirmation; the affidavit should give details of any such parties.[53] Directions (including the filing of pleadings, if appropriate) will then be given by the court. Otherwise, all creditors and members are bound by the scheme even if they did not attend the meeting or the hearing.

Non-Confirmation of Proposals

If the court refuses to confirm the proposals, it may decide simply to withdraw court protection without making any further order. But if it considers it fair and equitable to do so it may make an order for the winding-up of the company.[54] Rule 20 appears to envisage a separate application for the winding-up, though there is no reason why the court could not direct the examiner or such other person as it sees fit to make the application immediately. As the court has power to make any other order it sees fit, it presumably could also order the re-instatement of a receiver. In one case the proceedings were adjourned generally in order to allow an application brought by a creditor to have directors made personally liable for reckless trading to be heard.[55]

Breakdown of Scheme of Arrangement after Implementation

Many court-approved schemes of arrangement will require a company to

---

51.   Section 26.
52.   Section 27.
53.   Rule 21(1).
54.   Section24(11).
55.   In *Re Hefferon Kearns*, High Court (unreported), 14 December 1990 (*ex tempore*) (Costello J.). See also *Dublin Heating Company v Hefferon and Others* [1992] ILRM 51.

make a number of staged payments to various creditors. A company may succeed in paying the first dividend on time, but may delay or face difficulties in making subsequent payments. There is no reason why a creditor should not be able to sue the company in the event of such default. However, the company will only be liable for the balance of the dividend due to such a creditor under the approval scheme rather than the full amount which was due and owing by the company prior to the period of court protection. In certain circumstances, the court in approving the proposed scheme has also made an ancillary order that if the terms of the scheme are not complied with, certain creditors will be entitled to apply to court to have the company wound up, and to prove for the full amount originally due to them in the subsequent liquidation.[56] In view of the terms of section 24(6), a specific order granting such an entitlement is probably required.

Other rights which creditors may have against the company do not appear to be affected by the approval of a scheme of arrangement unless expressly extinguished or altered by court order. So a secured creditor retains the right to appoint a receiver (as well as other rights he may have under his debenture) in default of payment of the balance of the dividend due to him under the scheme. Creditors may also petition to have the company wound up in the ordinary way if their dividends are not paid. It is unclear whether or not the right of action under the Statute of Limitations 1957 accrues on the date of the approval by the court of the scheme, though any written acceptance of the examiner's report on the amounts due and the amounts which it is proposed to pay to creditors filed by the company at the hearing (e.g. in the form of a sworn affidavit) is likely to be regarded as an acknowledgment under that Act.[57]

56. In *Re 3V Multimedia Group* (footnote 4, above) the court directed that the Revenue Commissioners would be allowed to re-apply to have the company wound up and to prove for the full amount of taxes originally due if the company failed to pay its current taxes.

57. Section 56. See *Jones v Bellgrove Properties Ltd* [1949] 2 KB 700; *Re Overmark Smith Warden Ltd* [1982] 1 WLR 1195. Payment of a first dividend would probably constitute part payment under section 65.

CHAPTER 9

Reckless and Fraudulent Trading

Up to 1990 it was necessary to establish fraud on the part of directors and other officers in order to make them personally liable for the debts of the company. Such an application could only be made during a winding-up of the company. Fraudulent trading was also a criminal offence, though the penalties on conviction had become outdated. Section 33 and 34[1] of the Act (now expanded into sections 297A and 297 of the Principal Act) introduced radical changes to these mechanisms. Firstly, it is no longer necessary to establish fraud on the part of the persons concerned. Section 33 introduced the concept of reckless trading, which has a much lower threshold of impropriety. Secondly, an application to have directors made personally liable can be made whether or not the company is being wound up (though in practice the company must be unable to pay its debts as set out in section 214 of the Principal Act).[2] The penalties for the crime of fraudulent trading have been substantially increased.

While the time scale required for reckless trading or fraudulent trading proceedings makes it hard to imagine how such proceedings could be effectively maintained without defeating the prospects of a successful examinership, it is worth considering some of the aspects of these procedures in the context of a company under court protection.[3]

Reckless Trading

Under section 297A, an application (by motion on notice to the persons concerned) to have directors and others made personally liable for reckless trading may be made during the course of an examinership. As already pointed out, it is unlikely that an examiner would bring such an application as he would be unable to show the requisite loss or damage. The carrying

---

1. Repealed by section 180 and replaced by section 138 and 137 of the Companies Act 1990.
2. Section 297A(3).
3. For a more detailed consideration of reckless and fraudulent trading see Keane, 'Company Law in the Republic of Ireland', Butterworth (2nd ed., 1991) and Ussher, 'Company Law in Ireland', Sweet & Maxwell, (1986).

on of business by a company during the period of court protection is expressly declared not to be reckless under section 297A(8). However, a creditor or contributory may still have the appropriate *locus standi* to bring an application.

The concept and limits of reckless trading as set out in the section were explored in *Re Hefferon Kearns Ltd*.[4] A construction company which began trading in 1989 had sought and obtained court protection in October of 1990. The company had successfully reversed half-year losses by December of 1989, but delays in building, a dispute with one of the development site owners and the serious down-turn in the property market in the summer of 1990 left the company with a balance sheet deficit of over £142,000 in July of 1990. In August the directors decided to continue trading by giving priority to their most profitable contract, exercising tighter controls on costs and attempting to collect all monies due from debtors to discharge current creditors. By September it was clear that the company would have difficulty in continuing to pay current accounts and at a meeting at the end of the month (deferred from its original date because of the hospitalisation of one of the directors) it was decided to take other cost-cutting measures and to obtain a moratorium from all creditors. At the meeting of all the creditors on 11 October 1990, it was decided by a majority that an application for court protection should be made, which application was made the following day.

One of the creditors of the company was a small contractor. Owed in excess of £41,000, they claimed that the four directors and officers of the company had engaged in reckless trading by allowing creditors to believe that the company owned the sites on which they were building, by undercharging, by permitting works to be done by the company to the third defendant's house at a loss, and (in the case of the first and second named defendants) by benefiting through their shareholdings in the site-owning companies as a result of the company's losses. The examiner's proposed scheme of arrangement in December of 1990 was thus not implemented (despite support from a large number of other creditors) in order to allow the creditor to bring reckless trading proceedings against the four directors.

A number of issues were decided in a preliminary application before Murphy J.[5] He held that section 33(1)(a) could not be retrospective in effect having regard to constitutional and common law principles and presumptions, and the absence of any clearly declared intention of the legislature that the section was to be other than prospective. The liability (if any)

---

4.   [1992] ILRM 51. *Re Hefferon Kearns Ltd (No. 2)*, High Court (unreported), 14 January 1993 (Lynch J.).

5.   In *Re Hefferon Kearns; Dublin Heating Co v Hefferon and Others* [1992] ILRM 51.

of the directors would thus be confined to their behaviour from 29 August 1990 (the operative date on which the Act came into effect) to 12 October 1990 (the date on which the company came under the protection of the court). This would not mean that a court could not have regard to the behaviour or state of mind of the defendants prior to that period; but it did mean that any personal liability could only be imposed for debts incurred after 29 August. Murphy J. also held that the restriction in section 5(2)(f) of the Act which prevents proceedings being commenced against any person who is liable in respect of the debts of the company did not prevent application being made during the protection period in respect of earlier fraudulent or reckless trading. The apparent conflict between section 5(2)(f) (ii) and section 33 may be resolved by interpreting an application in respect of fraudulent or reckless trading as being proceedings in which the court decides on whether or not persons *should* be held liable for the company's debts, and are thus not proceedings against a person who *is* (already) liable, though Murphy J. described this as a 'refined distinction'.[6]

In the main action[7] Lynch J. held that the creditor had sustained loss and damage of £4,500 during the relevant period from 29 August to 11 October 1990. The insolvency of the company was not in dispute. He held that the creditor was not sufficiently aware of the company's financial state as to be affected by section 33(4) of the Act. On the substantive issues, Lynch J. held that the section did not impose a collective responsibility on the board of directors, but rather operated individually and personally on each of the officers and the onus of proof rested with the applicant in respect of each officer.

Citing the Supreme Court's analysis of the concept of recklessness in *Donovan v Landys Ltd*,[8] he held that the requirements of section 33(1)(a) that the officer in question was *knowingly* a party to the carrying on of the business must be intended to affect the nature of the reckless conduct coming within the sub-section. He held that such conduct would require knowledge on the part of the director of an obvious and serious risk of loss or damage to others, together with a deliberate ignoring of that risk (because of lack of care or selfishness). As two of the defendants had personally borrowed monies to improve the company's cash-flow, had personally guaranteed the company's debt with a bank and had traded in the (in the circumstances) not unreasonable belief that to do so would be better for the creditors than a liquidation, Lynch J. held that none of the defendants were

---

6.   At page 60.
7.   *Re Hefferon Kearns Ltd (No. 2) Dublin Heating Co Ltd v Hefferon and Others*, High Court (unreported), 14 January 1993 (Lynch J.).
8.   [1963] IR 441.

party to the carrying on of the business of the company in a reckless manner under section 33(1)(a). He also held that they did not know, nor ought to have known, that their actions or those of the company would cause loss to the creditors of the company. In an interesting analysis of section 33(2)(b) which deems a person to be knowingly party to the carrying on of business of the company in a reckless manner if that person was party to the contracting of a debt by the company and did not honestly believe on reasonable grounds that the company would be able to pay the debt when it fell due as well as all its other debts, he said that that the section 'appears to be a very wide ranging and indeed draconian measure and could apply in the case of virtually every company which becomes insolvent and has to cease trading for that reason'.[9] This, perhaps, was the reason for the inclusion of section 33(6) which allows a court to relieve from personal liability (in whole or part) a person who has acted honestly and responsibly in relation to the conduct of the affairs of the company. He thus held that while the first named defendant had been party to the contracting of debts by the company when he knew that those debts and all the other debts of the company could not be paid when they fell due, he should be wholly relieved from any personal liability without terms being imposed. In dismissing the claim, Lynch J. also held that the creditor had failed to prove that the loss sustained during the period was sustained *as a result* of the reckless trading, and that any diminution in the dividend which creditors would obtain in the liquidation was so trivial (ninety pounds) as not to be regarded as loss or damage under section 33(3)(b).

The judgment emphasises the requirement of actual (rather than imputed) guilty knowledge on the part of the director or officer for liability to be imposed under section 33(1)(a), thus distinguishing between reckless and negligent trading. The court may also be prepared to relieve from liability a director who was negligent (in that he ought to have known that loss would be caused to creditors) or who allowed the company to continue to incur debts if he at all times acted honestly and responsibly in relation to the affairs of the company and other related matters. So it appears that the circumstances in which personal liability will be imposed on a director or officer for reckless trading are narrower than might initially have been anticipated.[10] It seems the court will be slow to penalise directors or officers who have behaved honestly and responsibly unless there is evidence of

9.   Page 47 of the judgment.
10. Recklessness has been defined in the area of criminal law as the conscious disregard of a substantial and unjustifiable risk in circumstances where, having regard to the circumstances known to the person, such disregard involves culpability of a high degree. See *People (DPP) v Murray* [1977] IR 360. This is a subjective test; a stricter

gross disregard for the rights of others; misguided optimism of itself would not appear to contain the necessary element of moral turpitude.

Fraudulent Trading

Section 33 simply repeated the provisions of the old section 297(1) in respect of liability for fraudulent trading. As now enacted, an application to make any person (not just officers of the company) liable for the debts of the company can be made by a receiver, examiner, liquidator, creditor or contributory without the requirement that the applicant suffered loss as a result of the fraudulent trading. It is clear that an examiner would usually be the most appropriate person to bring such an application if such an application is to be made during an examinership.

However, there are considerable difficulties in proving the necessary intent to defraud which is required to establish fraudulent trading giving rise to personal liability. The deliberate falsification or destruction of financial documentation to hide the siphoning off of company assets to directors or elsewhere was held to be evidence of such an intent in *Re Aluminium Fabricators Ltd*[11] and in *Re Kelly's Carpetdrome Ltd.*[12] But a pattern of such fraudulent activity may not be necessary if a single transaction provides evidence of the requisite *mala fides*. In *Re Hunting Lodges Ltd*[13] the making of an 'under-the-table' payment (in addition to the purchase price paid for the company's principal asset, a pub) was held to be evidence of intent to defraud. The additional payment was never paid to the company, but disappeared into accounts held in fictitious names by the directors. The court imposed personal liability of varying degrees on the purchaser and his nominee company, as well as on the two directors. Proof of a conscious fraudulent purpose or intent will be difficult to establish in many, if not most, cases. Knowledge of irregularities or insolvent trading (without actual participation) is insufficient to attract liability, and financial advisers[14] and auditors[15] to companies have escaped liability in such circumstances. Perhaps it is the difficulty in discharging this strict onus of proof[16] which explains why there have been relatively few such actions in

'objective' test is used in English criminal law — *R. v Lawrence* [1982] AC 510; [1981] 2 WLR 524; [1981] 1 All ER 974.

11.   [1984] ILRM 399.
12.   High Court (unreported), 1 July 1983 (Costello J.).
13.   [1985] ILRM 75.
14.   *Re Maidstone Building Provisions Ltd* [1971] 1 WLR 1085.
15.   *Re Kelly's Carpetdrome Ltd (No. 2)* High Court (unreported), 13 July 1984 (O'Hanlon J.).
16.   As set out in *Hardie v Hanson* [1960] 105 CLR 451.

this jurisdiction.

In the event of any person or persons being found guilty of reckless or fraudulent trading, the court may declare them to be personally liable for all or any part of the debts or other liabilities of the company as the court shall direct. The sum (fixed) then becomes an asset of the company.[17] The court may also give further directions to give effect to such a declaration. For example, a director held personally liable may find that liability declared by the court to be a charge over any debt due by the company to him, and similar declarations can be made in respect of mortgages or charges in his favour on the assets of the company. The court can also provide for the enforcement of any such charges created by order; and it can also direct the payment of sums recovered to such classes of persons in such priorities and proportions as appears fit.[18] In *O'Keeffe v Ferris and Others*[19] it was contended that the language of the section, together with the mental element of the wrongdoing required and the sanction which could be imposed meant that in effect the section created a criminal offence. Rejecting this argument, Murphy J., noted that a number of the indicia of a criminal offence identified by the Supreme Court in *Melling v O'Mathghamhna*[20] were absent from the section or else were only present in ambiguous form. The State was not identified as the party who could commence or terminate proceedings. The body of creditors (rather than the State) was the injured party. Proceedings could only be commenced if the company was in liquidation (or, since 1990, in examinership), a limitation which would seem extraordinary if the fraud in question was deemed to be a crime. Observing that the use of words such as 'fraud' or 'with intent to defraud' are not uncommon in civil proceedings, Murphy J. held there was an extraordinary 'dearth of terms which one would expect to find in a sub-section dealing with a criminal offence'.[21] In this respect the section was in marked contrast to what is now section 297, which clearly created the criminal offence and provided for the manner and extent to which it was to be punished.

While it was clearly unusual that the section provided that any monies recovered were to be distributed amongst the body of the creditors (rather than retained by, for example, the individual creditor who had instituted the proceedings) Murphy J. held that the section contemplated a form of a class or representative action which could be invoked so as to recover compensation from a group of wrongdoers for the benefit of those who are

17.   Section 297A(1). See *Re William C. Leitch Bros Ltd. (No. 2)* [1993] Ch. 261.
18.   Section 297A(7).
19.   High Court (unreported), 28 July 1993 (Murphy J.).
20.   [1963] IR 1.   21. At page 11 of the judgment.

wronged. Undoubtedly the power to fix a person with unlimited liability for the debts of a company is extraordinarily wide; it certainly does not conform to the popular notion of compensation in civil proceedings. Noting the wide discretion conferred on the Court by the section in this respect, Murphy J. held that 'it must be assumed that the Court will exercise those powers, not merely in a responsible but also in a constitutional fashion.[22]

O'Keeffe v Ferris and Others decides that the section creates a civil rather than a criminal offence. However, it is uncertain which standard of proof is applicable to proceedings under the section. In *Re Kelly's Carpet-drome*[23] Costello J. utilized both criminal and civil standards in concluding that the defendants should be made liable, while in *Re Kelly's Carpetdrome (No. 2)*[24] O'Hanlon held that the auditors should be exonerated by either standard of proof. The section expressly states that a finding of reckless or fraudulent trading (and consequent liability for the debts of the company) shall have effect even if the person is *also* criminally liable in respect of the same matters,[25] which may imply that the civil standard of proof is sufficient. But it is the extent of the sanction that may be imposed by the court which gives rise to the concern that the section may be constitutionally unsound, since it provides for the trial of a matter which is essentially criminal without the attendant rights and guarantees set out in Article 38 and elsewhere in the Constitution.

Fraudulent Trading: Criminal Liability

Section 297 maintains the criminal offence (created in section 297(3) of the Principal Act) of fraudulent trading. Dishonesty amounting to an intent to defraud must be proved beyond reasonable doubt to establish the offence.[26] Any person knowingly party to the carrying on of the business of the company with intent to defraud the creditors of the company, or creditors of any other person or for any other fraudulent purpose is guilty. Such a person is liable on summary conviction to imprisonment for a term not exceeding 12 months or to a fine not exceeding £1,000 or both, and on indictment to imprisonment for a term not exceeding seven years or a fine not exceeding £50,000 or both. It is not a prerequisite for a prosecution under the section that the company be insolvent. To date no successful prosecutions have taken place; the difficulties in proving the required intent

22.   At page 1 of the judgment. The decision is under appeal.
23.   Footnote 12 above.
24.   Footnote 15 above.
25.   Section 297A(9).
26.   *R. v Cox & Hedges* [1982] Cr App R 291 (CA); *R. v Ghosh* [1982] QB 1053.

to defraud in accordance with the criminal standard of proof undoubtedly deter the authorities to an extent.

Misfeasance, Breach of Duty and Breach of Trust

Section 298 extends and re-enacts the power (originally granted by section 298 of the Principal Act) of the court to assess damages against directors, officers and liquidators, receivers or examiners of companies. The section does not create new rights or liabilities,[27] but rather provides a summary procedure whereby the wrong-doings of any such person in relation to a company may be remedied. In including receivers and examiners, the new section 298 widens the net; it is also clear that the inclusion of liability for breach of duty is intended to remedy the former position whereby the section was held to exclude the *negligence* of former officers.[28] The section applies during a winding-up and is invoked by an application to court of the liquidator, a creditor or contributory. It is necessary to show that actual pecuniary loss has been suffered by the company.[29] No proceedings under this section have been brought against an examiner to date.

---

27. *Re Irish Provident Assurance Co* [1913] 1 IR 352.
28. In *Re B. Johnson & Co. Builders Ltd* [1955] Ch. 634.
29. *Re J.M. Barker Ltd* [1950] IR 123.

CHAPTER 10

Remuneration, Costs and Expenses

The examiner is an officer of the court whose appointment and termination is determined by court order. As with liquidators, his remuneration, costs and expenses are sanctioned by the court before they are paid under section 29 of the Act. An application for sanction and payment of remuneration, costs and expenses is usually made by an examiner at the conclusion of the examinership, though as we have seen[1] the court has power to limit the expenses which the examiner may certify at a much earlier stage if it thinks it proper to do so. Because of the short time scale of examinerships there is no provision or practical necessity for payments on account.

Section 29 provides that unless otherwise ordered by the court, the remuneration costs and expenses of the examiner shall be paid out of the revenue of the company or the proceeds of realisation of the company's assets. More importantly, the remuneration costs and expenses sanctioned by the court are given priority over other debts owed by the company. Section 29(3) provides that sanctioned remuneration, costs and expenses shall be paid before any other claim (whether secured or unsecured) under any compromise, scheme of arrangement, receivership or winding-up of the company. The examiner will thus rank ahead of preferential creditors or fixed-charge holders. This priority has led the courts to be vigilant in scrutinising an examiner's application for sanction and payment.

That the court has jurisdiction to review and disallow the remuneration, costs and expenses of the examiner is clear from the wording of the section itself, and from recent decisions concerning its interpretation. The section allows the court to make such orders 'as it thinks proper' for the payment of the amounts sought. The reference to 'reasonable expenses properly incurred by the examiner' thus permits a court to consider both the quantum of the expenses incurred and certified as well as their propriety. The court also appears to be empowered to order that the remuneration, costs and

---

1.   See chapter 4. See also *Re Don Bluth Entertainment Ltd (No. 1)*, High Court (unreported), 27 August 1992 (Murphy J.).

expenses of the examiner not be paid from the revenue of the business of the company. It is hard to envisage a situation whereby some party other than the company would be ordered to discharge the amounts sought; but it has been held that the section empowers the court to refuse to order payment of the amount sought.

In *Re Wogan's (Drogheda) Ltd (No. 3)*[2] the examiner applied for sanction and payment of the remuneration costs and expenses incurred by him in the course of the examinership. The court had previously[3] refused to confirm a scheme of arrangement proposed by him, ordering instead that the company be wound up. One of the reasons given for the court's refusal to confirm was that a significant abuse of process of the court had taken place at the time of the presentation of the petition. The court held that the examiner's concealment of inaccuracies in the petition together with his failure to take steps to ascertain the true position at that time amounted to a breach of his duty to the court. He also failed at the time of the petition to inform the court that he had acted for the company prior to his appointment, and also as an 'informal' interim examiner. Costello J. held that these were serious breaches of duty, and in the circumstances it would be unjust for the company's creditors to remunerate or indemnify him. In part this ruling was based on the view that it was 'highly probable' that had these matters been disclosed to the courts at the time, the protection order and appointment of the examiner would not have been made. He also emphasised again the duties and responsibilities of professional persons to the court, particularly the requirement that they exercise utmost good faith.

Costello J. also held that the presence of numerous serious defects in the proposed scheme of arrangement were such that it would be unjust to ask creditors to remunerate and indemnify him out of company assets. The formation of the scheme of arrangement was only one aspect of the unsatisfactory conduct by him of the examinership.

The manner in which the examiner conducted the examinership was also the subject of scrutiny in *Re Clare Textiles Ltd*.[4] In that case the examiner proposed a scheme of arrangement whereby the company's premises and business, stock and machinery would be sold to different purchasers. While a limited number of employees would be retained by one of these purchasers, the company itself would cease to trade. The court refused to confirm this scheme, holding that the formulation of proposals for a scheme of arrangement should only take place where the examiner has concluded in his first report that the company *and* the whole or any part of its

2.   High Court (unreported), 9 February 1993 (Costello J.).
3.   High Court (unreported), 7 May 1992 (Costello J.).
4.   [1993] 2 IR 213.

undertaking were capable of survival as a going concern. Since the company was not surviving, this was in effect a liquidation. Costello J. held that the examiner should only be allowed his remuneration and legal costs up to the date on which he ceased to properly carry out his statutory duty (being the period prior to the delivery of his first report). To allow remuneration and costs for any further period during which the examiner was performing unauthorised functions resulting from what was in effect an error of construction of the Act would not, he held, be proper or fair to the creditors of the company.

In both cases the examiner's application for sanction and payment was opposed by creditors of the company, which in both cases was insolvent and in liquidation. The priority granted by section 20(3) (which does not appear to be capable of variation by the court) in such circumstances will usually impinge on the likelihood of creditors of the company being paid, whether in full or at all. In such cases the court will be concerned to ensure that an examiner's impropriety or wrong-doing is not rewarded by the discharging of his remuneration and legal costs at the expense of other creditors. An Examiner has also been disallowed a proportion of his remuneration where the Court took the view that the examination of the company should have been concluded sooner[4a] although the Court is usually unwilling to rely too heavily on the benefit of hindsight in coming to such a conclusion.[4b]

The question of 'expenses' is more difficult. Traditionally, expenses are understood to refer to outlay and other miscellaneous expenses incurred by the examiner himself. But section 10 of the Act provides that liabilities of the company certified by the examiner as being necessarily and properly incurred for the survival of the company during the protection period are also to be treated as expenses. An examiner in his section 29 application will usually seek payment not only of monies due to himself, but also of those monies due to creditors of the company which he has certified. As previously indicated, the certification process radically alters the priority of debt which would otherwise apply in insolvency. To prevent a dilution of their own entitlements secured creditors may therefore seek to challenge the sanction and payment of certified expenses under section 10.

The extent to which a court can review the certification by the examiner of a liability as an expense was considered in *Re Don Bluth Entertainment Ltd (No. 2)*.[5] A petition for protection presented by the directors of the

4a. *Re Edenpark Construction*, High Court (unreported), 17 December 1993 (Murphy J.).
4b. Re *Bernard McDevitt & Co. Ltd*, High Court (unreported), 9 July 1993 (Murphy J.). See also *Mellor v Mellor and Others* [1992] 4 All ER 10 at 18.
5. High Court (unreported), 24 May 1993 (Murphy J.).

company was granted by the court. Between the date of the presentation and the hearing of the petition an interim examiner had been appointed who had certified a number of liabilities as expenses under section 10. In particular, liabilities due to a firm of solicitors in connection with the presentation and hearing of the petition were certified. The certification of this expense was challenged by the bank which, although unsecured, had provided con- siderable finance to the company in the past.

The court held that it could review the certification of a liability by the examiner as an expense under section 10. Declining to apply by analogy the principles applicable to a judicial review of an administrative decision, the court instead appeared to rely on the use of the words 'may' and 'reasonable' in section 29 as conferring a discretion in respect of sanctioning payment, as well as a function in determining whether expenses had been incurred reasonably or otherwise. The existence of such a discretion also appears to have been implicitly accepted in *Re Clare Textiles Ltd.*[6] As a result, the court has power (i) to review the validity of the certificate issued, (ii) to consider whether or not the expenses certified were reasonable, and (iii) to consider whether or not reasonable expenses validly certified should be paid. It is likely, however, that once the certificate has been sanctioned as valid and reasonable the court will order that the liability which it certifies be paid. Such a payment must be in accordance with the priority set out in section 29(3); the court appears to have no jurisdiction to vary the order of payment under the section.

In *Re Don Bluth Entertainment Ltd (No. 2)*[7] the court held that the petition presented by the directors was in reality a petition presented on behalf of the company, and therefore that the liabilities certified to the solicitors were liabilities in respect of services provided at the request of and for the benefit of the company itself. It will be recalled, however, that the Act confers no priority on the costs of persons petitioning for the appointment of an examiner. The court held that it would be inappropriate to alter the scheme of the Act by permitting an interim examiner fortuitously appointed to certify the petitioners' costs where the legislation had withheld such a priority. In so far as the certificate related to liabilities already incurred prior to his appointment (in the presentation of the petition), it was held to be of no statutory effect. The court also held that the certification of contemporaneous liabilities in respect of proceedings for the appointment of an examiner (i.e. the hearing of the petition) was invalid. Since the protection period during which the survival of the company falls to be

6.   See footnote 4 above.
7.   High Court (unreported), 24 May 1993 (Murphy J.).

considered is a period which commences with and postulates the existence of an examiner, it was held that the proceedings leading to the appointment of an examiner could have no bearing on the survival of the company during the relevant period. In essence, the court refused to sanction as reasonable expenses liabilities for costs associated with the presentation of the petition and the appointment of an examiner. It is thus now clear that a petitioner cannot recover the costs of presenting the petition in priority under the certification procedure;[8] he is also unlikely to recover them by way of an order for costs (except perhaps in extraordinary circumstances). Whether this will discourage parties from presenting petitions remains to be seen.

The court had no difficulty in sanctioning the other liabilities incurred in respect of the day-to-day services and advice provided by the solicitors to the company during the protection period, while directing taxation of the bill in question.

Two other matters arose relating to expenses in the case. A bank who had been the principal source of finance to the company prior to the petition advanced a substantial sum to the company, which was certified. The certificate made no express provision in respect of interest, and indeed there was no documentation which recorded the precise terms of the advance. However, the court upheld the claim by the bank that implicit in the transaction was the term that the advance would carry interest in the same way as previous advances made. Accordingly, the court sanctioned repayment of the advance with interest thereon.

The other issue was the date on which liabilities incurred in US dollars should be translated into Irish currency. Because the company was now in liquidation, it was held that the conversion date should be the date of the presentation of the petition to wind up the company,[9] being the date on which the liquidator (rather than the company) becomes responsible for the discharge of expenses certified and sanctioned. Such interest as was payable on the debts after the commencement of the liquidation would be paid on the converted sum.

Procedure

While the rules provide[10] that the examiner's application for action and payment is made *ex parte*, in practice the company will usually be notified. If the examinership has been unsuccessful and the company has gone into

8.   See *In Re Merrytime (Ireland) Ltd*, High Court (unreported), 29 June 1992 (*ex tempore*) (Murphy J.).

9.   Following *Re Lines Bros Ltd* [1982] 2 WLR page 1010.

10.   Rule 22.

liquidation or receivership, it is appropriate (and the court may so direct) that the liquidator or receiver be a notice-party as well as such other persons (e.g. certain large secured or unsecured creditors) as may seem fit. Directions as to service and the date of the hearing of the application may then be given.

The examiner's application is grounded on affidavit. He should specify in his affidavit what use, if any, he has made of the services of staff and/or facilities of the company in carrying out his functions. Section 29(4) obliges the examiner to make as much use as is reasonably possible of such services of staff and facilities (presumably in an attempt to reduce costs) and the court must have particular regard to this provision in considering the application of the examiner.[11]

Otherwise the format of the examiner's affidavit should be similar to that used in a fee application by a liquidator in a winding-up by the court. As well as setting out in detail the progress of the examinership and the work carried out by him and his staff, the examiner should exhibit a specific breakdown of the fees and hourly rates charged by him. He should also vouch any outlay where possible. In dealing with the expenses certified by him under section 10 during the protection period, the examiner should exhibit copies of the certificates together with the correspondence and other documentation relevant to the issuing of each certificate. It may also be appropriate to explain the reasons for certifying these expenses in the course of the affidavit.

There is no requirement that the examiner's legal fees be taxed prior to the application. Frequently the court will order taxation if the fees are substantial or if other notice-parties request this. It has been stated[12] that the bill should be prepared in the usual manner as if for presentation to a taxing-master. A letter from a cost drawer approving the fees charged may be of assistance.

Costs

Prima facie the examiner would appear to be entitled to his costs of the application against the company, though where there are no notice-parties the issue will in practice have been agreed between the examiner and the company prior to the application. But the court has a wide discretion in the matter. In *Re Wogans (Drogheda) Ltd (No. 3)*[13] Costello J. refused the examiner's application in its entirety, and also refused to grant the examiner

11. Company 29(4).
12. See *Re Clare Textiles Ltd*, footnote 4 above.
13. Footnote 2 above.

his costs. In that case creditors who had opposed the application (and indeed the petition) sought to have their costs paid by the directors, the company, or the examiner. Costello J. held that their costs did not constitute debts or other liabilities of the company under section 297A. As the directors were not parties to any of the proceedings, he refused to award the costs against them. He also refused to award costs against the company as the liability of the company for the directors' wrong-doing was far from clear and to do so would be unfair to the company's unsecured creditors. Section 29 of the Act does not appear to empower the court to make an order in favour of creditors against the directors, the company or the examiner. But order 99(I)(1) does confer power to make orders relating to costs incurred by parties who appeared at the proceedings. Costello J. held that the interests of justice did not require him to make an order that the examiner should pay the creditors' costs in the present case, though he acknowledged that such an order might be made in exceptional circumstances.[14]

14.   In *Re Wogans (Drogheda) Ltd (No. 3)* an allegation by the examiner that the receiver 'had deliberately distorted the price obtained by him for property so as to prevent or make it difficult for the examiner to get paid his remuneration costs and expenses' was held to be groundless. The receiver was awarded his costs against the examiner.

APPENDIX I

Companies (Amendment) Act 1990
(as amended)
by sections 180 and 181 of The Companies (No. 2) Act, 1990)
Number 27 *of* 1990

1. —In this Act, unless the context otherwise requires— *[Definitions]*

"the Companies Act" means the Principal Act, and every enactment (including this Act) which is to be construed as one with that Act;

"examiner" means an examiner appointed under *section 2*;

"interested party", in relation to a company to which *section 2(1)* relates, means—
(*a*) a creditor of the company;
(*b*) a member of the company;

"the Minister" means the Minister for Industry and Commerce;

"the Principal Act" means the Companies Act, 1963.

subject to as.(2)

2.—(1) Where it appears to the court that— *[Power of court to appoint examiner (amended)]*
(*a*) a company is or is likely to be unable to pay its debts, and
(*b*) no resolution subsists for the winding-up of the company, and
(*c*) no order has been made for the winding-up of the company,

it may, on application by petition presented, appoint an examiner to the company for the purpose of examining the state of the company's affairs and performing such duties in relation to the company as may be imposed by or under this Act.

(2) ~~Without prejudice to the general power of~~ the court under ~~subsection (1), it~~ *shall* ~~may, in particular, make~~ *not* an order under this section ~~if it considers that such order~~ *into is satisfied that there* ~~would be likely to facilitate~~ the survival of the company, and the whole or in *any* part *is a* of its undertaking, as a going concern. *reasonable prospect*

(3) For the purpose of this section, a company is unable to pay its debts if—
(*a*) it is unable to pay its debts as they fall due;
(*b*) the value of its assets is less than the amount of its liabilities, taking into account its contingent and prospective liabilities, or
(*c*) section 214(*a*) and (*b*) of the Principal Act applies to the company.

(4) In deciding whether to make an order under this section the court may also have regard to whether the company has sought from its creditors significant extensions of time for the payment of its debts, from which it could reasonably be inferred that the company was likely to be unable to pay its debts.

Petition
for
protection
of the
court
(amended

3.—(1) Subject to *subsection (2)*, a petition under *section 2* may be presented by—

    (*a*) the company, or

    (*b*) the directors of the company, or

    (*c*) a creditor, or contingent or prospective creditor (including an employee) of the company, or

    (*d*) members of the company holding at the date of the presentation of a petition under that section not less than one-tenth of such of the paid-up capital of the company as carries at that date the right of voting at general meetings of the company,

or by all or any of those parties, together or separately.

    (2)   (*a*) Where the company referred to in *section 2* is an insurer, a petition under that section may be presented only by the Minister, and *subsection (1)* of this section shall not apply to the company,

        (*b*) Where the company referred to in *section 2* is the holder of a licence under section 9 by the Central Bank Act, 1971, or any other company supervised by the Central Bank under any enactment, a petition under *section 2* may be presented only by the Central Bank, and *subsection (1)* of this section shall not apply to the company.

    (3) A petition presented under *section 2* shall—

    (*a*) nominate a person to be appointed as examiner, and

    (*b*) be supported by such evidence as the court may require for the purpose of showing that the petitioner has good reason for requiring the appointment of an examiner, and

    (*c*) where the petition is presented by any person or persons referred to in *subsection (1)(a)* or *(b)*, include a statement of the assets and liabilities of the company (in so far as they are known to them) as they stand on a date not earlier than 7 days before the presentation of the petition.

    (4) A petition presented under *section 2* shall be accompanied—

    (*a*) by a consent signed by the person nominated to be examiner, and

    (*b*) if proposals for a compromise or scheme of arrangement in relation to the company's affairs have been prepared for submission to interested parties for their approval, by a copy of the proposals.

    (5) The court shall not give a hearing to a petition under *section 2* presented by a contingent or prospective creditor until such security for costs has been given as the court thinks reasonable, and until a prima facie case for the protection of the court has been established to the satisfaction of the court.

    (6) The court shall not give a hearing to a petition under *section 2* if a receiver stands appointed to the company the subject of the petition and such receiver has stood so appointed for a continuous period of at least [3 days] prior to the presentation of the petition.

    (7) On hearing a petition under this section, the court may dismiss it, or adjourn the hearing conditionally or unconditionally, or make any interim order, or any other order it thinks fit.

(8) Without prejudice to the generality of *subsection (7)*, an interim order under that subsection may restrict the exercise of any powers of the directors or of the company (whether by reference to the consent of the court or otherwise).

(9) (*a*) Where it appears to the court that the total liabilities of the company (taking into account its contingent and prospective liabilities) do not exceed £250,000, the court may, after making such interim or other orders as it thinks fit, order that the matter be remitted to the judge of the Circuit Court in whose circuit the company has its registered office or principal place of business.

(*b*) Where an order is made by the court under this subsection the Circuit Court shall have full jurisdiction to exercise all the powers of the court conferred by this Act in relation to the company and every reference to the court in this Act shall be construed accordingly.

(*c*) Where, in any proceedings under this Act which have been remitted to the Circuit Court by virtue of this subsection, it appears to the Circuit Court that the total liabilities of the company exceed £250,000, it shall make, after making such interim orders as it thinks fit, an order transferring the matter to the court.

4.—(1) Where the court appoints an examiner to a company, it may, at the same or any time thereafter, make an order—

(*a*) appointing the examiner to be examiner for the purposes of this Act to a related company, or

(*b*) conferring on the examiner, in relation to such company, all or any of the powers or duties conferred on him in relation to the first-mentioned company.

Related companies (amended)

(2) In deciding whether to make an order under *subsection (1)*, the court shall have regard to whether the making of the order would be likely to facilitate the survival of the company, or of the related companies, or both, and the whole or any part of its or their undertaking, as a going concern.

(3) A related company to which an examiner is appointed shall be deemed to be under the protection of the court for the period beginning on the date of the making of an order under this section and continuing for the period during which the company to which it is related is under such protection.

(4) Where an examiner stands appointed to two or more related companies, he shall have the same powers and duties in relation to each company, taken separately, unless the court otherwise directs.

(5) For the purposes of this Act, a company is related to another company if—

(*a*) that other company is its holding company or subsidiary; or

(*b*) more than half in nominal value of its equity share capital (as defined in section 155(5) of the Principal Act) is held by the other company and companies related to that other company (whether directly or indirectly, but other than in a fiduciary capacity); or

(c) more than half in nominal value of the equity share capital (as defined in section 155(5) of the Principal Act) of each of them is held by members of the other (whether directly of indirectly, but other than in a fiduciary capacity); or

(*d*) that other company or a company or companies related to that other company or that other company together with a company or companies related to it are entitled to exercise or control the exercise of more than one half of the voting power at any general meeting of the company; or

(*e*) the businesses of the companies have been so carried on that the separate business of each company, or a substantial part thereof, is not readily identifiable; or

(*f*) there is another body corporate to which both companies are related;

and "related company" has a corresponding meaning.

(6) For the purposes of this section "company" includes any body which is liable to be wound up under the Companies Acts.

Effect of petition to appoint examiner on creditors and others (amended)

5.—(1) During the period beginning with the presentation of a petition for the appointment of an examiner to a company and (subject to *section 18(3)* or *(4)*) ending on the expiry of three months from that date or on the withdrawal or refusal of the petition, whichever first happens, the company shall be deemed to be under the protection of the court.

(2) For so long as a company is under the protection of the court in a case under this Act, the following provisions shall have effect—

(*a*) no proceedings for the winding-up of the company may be commenced or resolution for winding-up passed in relation to that company and any resolution so passed shall be of no effect;

(*b*) no receiver over any part of the property or undertaking of the company shall be appointed, or, if so appointed before the presentation of a petition under *section 2*, shall, subject to *section 6*, be able to act;

(*c*) no attachment, sequestration, distress or execution shall be put into force against the property or effects of the company, except with the consent of the examiner;

(*d*) where any claim against the company is secured by a charge on the whole or any part of the property, effects or income of the company, no action may be taken to realise the whole or any part of such security, except with the consent of the examiner;

(*e*) no steps may be taken to repossess goods in the company's possession under any hire-purchase agreement (within the meaning of *section 11(8)*), except with the consent of the examiner;

(*f*) where, under any enactment, rule of law or otherwise, any person other than the company is liable to pay all or any part of the debts of the company—

(i) no attachment, sequestration, distress or execution shall be put into force against the property or effects of such person in respect of the debts of the company, and

(ii) no proceedings of any sort may be commenced against such person in respect of the debts of the company.

[(g) no order for relief shall be made under section 205 of the Principal Act against the company in respect of complaints as to the conduct of the affairs of the company or the exercise of the powers of the directors prior to the presentation of the petition.]

[(h) no set-off between separate bank accounts of the company shall be effected, except with the consent of the examiner, and in this paragraph "bank account" includes an account with any person exempt by virtue of section 7(4) of the Central Bank Act, 1971, from the requirement of holding a licence under section 9 of that Act.]

(3) Subject to *subsection (2)*, no other proceedings in relation to the company may be commenced except by leave of the court and subject to such terms as the court may impose and the court may on the application of the examiner make such order as it thinks proper in relation to any existing proceedings including an order to stay such proceedings.

(4) Complaints concerning the conduct of the affairs of the company while it is under the protection of the court shall not constitute a basis for the making of an order for relief under section 205 of the Principal Act.

6.—(1) Where the court appoints an examiner to a company and a receiver stands appointed to the whole or any part of the property or undertaking of that company the court may make such order as it thinks fit including an order as to any or all of the following matters— *Effect on receiver or provisional liquidator of order appointing examiner*

(a) that the receiver shall cease to act as such from a date specified by the court,

(b) that the receiver shall, from a date specified by the court, act as such only in respect of certain assets specified by the court,

(c) directing the receiver to deliver all books, papers and other records, which relate to the property or undertaking of the company (or any part thereof) and are in his possession or control, to the examiner within a period to be specified by the court.

(d) directing the receiver to give the examiner full particulars of all his dealings with the property or undertaking of the company.

(2) Where the court appoints an examiner to a company and a provisional liquidator stands appointed to that company, the court may make such order as it thinks fit including an order as to any or all of the following matters—

(a) that the provisional liquidator be appointed as examiner of the company,

(b) appointing some other person as examiner of the company,

(c) that the provisional liquidator shall cease to act as such from the date specified by the court,

(d) directing the provisional liquidator to deliver all books, papers and other records, which relate to the property or undertaking of the company, or any part thereof and are in his possession or control, to the examiner within a period to be specified by the court,

(*e*) directing the provisional liquidator to give the examiner full particulars of all his dealings with the property or undertaking of the company.

(3) In deciding whether to make an order under *subsection (1)(a)* or *(b)*, or *subsection (2)(c)*, the court shall have regard to whether the making of the order would be likely to facilitate the survival of the company, and the whole or any part of its undertaking, as a going concern.

(4) Where the court makes an order under *subsection (1)* or *(2)*, it may, for the purpose of giving full effect to the order, include such conditions in the order and make such ancillary or other orders as it deems fit.

(5) Where a petition is presented under *section 2* in respect of a company at a date subsequent to the presentation of a petition for the winding-up of that company, but before a provisional liquidator has been appointed or an order made for its winding-up, both petitions shall be heard together.

Powers of an examiner

7.—(1) Any provision of the Companies Acts relating to the rights and powers of an auditor of a company and the supplying of information to and co-operation with such auditor shall, with the necessary modifications, apply to an examiner.

(2) Notwithstanding any provision of the Companies Acts relating to notice of general meetings, an examiner shall have power to convene, set the agenda for, and preside at meetings of the board of directors and general meetings of the company to which he is appointed and to propose motions or resolutions and to give reports to such meetings.

(3) An examiner shall be entitled to reasonable notice of, to attend and be heard at, all meetings of the board of directors of a company and all general meetings of the company to which he is appointed.

(4) For the purpose of *subsection (3)* "reasonable notice" shall be deemed to include a description of the business to be transacted at any such meeting.

(5) Where an examiner becomes aware of any actual or proposed act, omission, course of conduct, decision or contract, by or on behalf of the company to which he has been appointed, its officers, employees, members or creditors or by any other person in relation to the income, assets or liabilities of that company which, in his opinion, is or is likely to be to the detriment of the company, or any interested party, he shall, subject to the rights of parties acquiring an interest in good faith and for value in such income, assets or liabilities, have full power to take whatever steps are necessary to halt, prevent or rectify the effects of such act, omission, course of conduct, decision or contract.

(6) The examiner may apply to the court to determine any question arising in the course of his office, or for the exercise in relation to the company of all or any of the powers which the court may exercise under this Act, upon the application to it of any member, contributory, creditor or director of a company.

(7) The examiner shall, if so directed by the court, have power to ascertain and agree claims against the company to which he has been appointed.

8.—(1) It shall be the duty of all officers and agents of the company or a related company to produce to the examiner all books and documents of or relating to any such company which are in their custody or power, to attend before him when required so to do and otherwise to give to him all assistance in connection with his functions which they are reasonably able to give.

(2) If the examiner considers that a person other than an officer or agent of any such company is or may be in possession of any information concerning his affairs, he may require that person to produce to him any books or documents in his custody or power relating to the company, to attend before him and otherwise to give him all assistance in connection with his functions which he is reasonably able to give; and it shall be the duty of that person to comply with the requirement.

(3) If the examiner has reasonable grounds for believing that a director . . . of any such company maintains or has maintained a bank account of any description, whether alone or jointly with another person and whether in the State or elsewhere, into or out of which there has been paid—

> (*a*) any money which has resulted from or been used in the financing of any transaction, arrangement or agreement particulars of which have not been disclosed in the accounts of any company for any financial year as required by law; or
>
> (*b*) any money which has been in any way connected with any act or omission, or series of acts or omissions, which on the part of that director constituted misconduct (whether fraudulent or not) towards that company or its members;

the examiner may require the director to produce to him all documents in the director's possession, or under his control, relating to that bank account; and in this subsection "bank account" includes an account with any person exempt by virtue of section 7(4) of the Central Bank Act, 1971, from the requirement of holding a licence under section 9 of that Act [and "director" includes any present or past director or any person connected, within the meaning of *section 26* of the *Companies Act, 1990*, with such director, and any present or past shadow director].

(4) An examiner may examine on oath, either by word of mouth or on written interrogatories, the officers and agents of such company or other person as is mentioned in *subsection (1)* or *(2)* in relation to its affairs and may—

> (*a*) administer an oath accordingly,
>
> (*b*) reduce the answers of such person to writing and require him to sign them.

(5) If any officer or agent of such company or other person refuses to produce to the examiner any book or document which it is his duty under this section so to produce, refuses to attend before the examiner when required so to do or refuses to answer any question which is put to him by the examiner with respect to the affairs of the company, the examiner may certify the refusal under this hand to the court, and the court may thereupon enquire into the case and, after hearing any witnesses who may be produced against or on behalf of the alleged offender and any statement which may be offered in defence, punish the offender in like manner as if he had been guilty of contempt of court.

Production of documents and evidence (amended)

[(5A) Without prejudice to its power under subsection (5), the court may, after a hearing under that subsection, make any order or direction it thinks fit, including a direction to the person concerned to attend or re-attend before the examiner or produce particular books or documents or answer particular questions put to him by the examiner, or a direction that the person concerned need not produce a particular book or document or answer a particular question put to him by the examiner.

(5B) *Section 23(1)* of the *Companies Act, 1990* shall apply for the purposes of this section.]

(6) In this section, any reference to officers or to agents shall include past, as well as present, officers or agents, as the case may be, and "agents", in relation to a company, shall include the bankers and solicitors of the company and any person employed by the company as auditors, whether those persons are or are not officers of the company.

Further powers of court

9.—(1) Where it appears to the court, on the application of the examiner, that, having regard to the matters referred to in *subsection (2)*, it is just and equitable to do so, it may make an order that all or any of the functions or powers which are vested in or exercisable by the directors (whether by virtue of the memorandum or articles of association of the company or by law or otherwise) shall be performable or exercisable only by the examiner.

(2) The matters to which the court is to have regard for the purpose of *subsection(1)* are—

(*a*) that the affairs of the company are being conducted, or are likely to be conducted, in a manner which is calculated or likely to prejudice the interests of the company or of its employees or of its creditors as a whole, or

(*b*) that it is expedient, for the purpose of preserving the assets of the company or of safeguarding the interests of the company or of its employees or of its creditors as a whole, that the carrying on of the business of the company by, or the exercise of the powers of, its directors or management should be curtailed or regulated in any particular respect, or

(*c*) that the company, or its directors, have resolved that such an order should be sought, or

(*d*) any other matter in relation to the company the court thinks relevant.

(3) Where the court makes an order under *subsection (1)*, it may, for the purpose of giving full effect to the order, include such conditions in the order and make such ancillary or other orders as it sees fit.

(4) Without prejudice to the generality of *subsections (1)* and *(3)*, an order under this section may provide that the examiner shall have all or any of the powers that he would have if he were a liquidator appointed by the court in respect of the company and, where such order so provides, the court shall have all the powers that it would have if it had made a winding-up order and appointed a liquidator in respect of the company concerned.

10.—(1) [Any] liabilities incurred by the company during the protection period which are referred to in *subsection (2)* shall be treated as expenses properly incurred, for the purpose of *section 29*, by the examiner.

(2) The liabilities referred to in *subsection (1)* are those certified by the examiner at the time they are incurred, to have been incurred in circumstances where, in the opinion of the examiner, the survival of the company as a going concern during the protection period would otherwise be seriously prejudiced.

(3) In this section "protection period" means the period, beginning with the appointment of an examiner, during which the company is under the protection of the court.

Incurring of certain liabilities by examiner (amended)

11.—(1) Where, on an application by the examiner, the court is satisfied that the disposal (with or without other assets) of any property of the company which is subject to a security which, as created, was a floating charge or the exercise of his powers in relation to such property would be likely to facilitate the survival of the whole or any part of the company as a going concern, the court may by order authorise the examiner to dispose of the property, or exercise his powers in relation to it, as the case may be, as if it were not subject to the security.

Power to deal with charged property, etc. (amended)

(2) Where, on an application by the examiner, the court is satisfied that the disposal (with or without other assets) of—

        (*a*) any property of the company subject to a security other than a security to which *subsection (1)* applies, or

        (*b*) any goods in the possession of the company under a hire-purchase agreement,

would be likely to facilitate the survival of the whole or any part of the company as a going concern, the court may by order authorise the examiner to dispose of the property as if it where not subject to the security or to dispose of the goods as if all rights of the owner under the hire-purchase agreement were vested in the company.

(3) Where property is disposed of under *subsection (1)*, the holder of the security shall have the same priority in respect of any property of the company directly or indirectly representing the property disposed of as he would have had in respect of the property subject to the security.

(4) It shall be a condition of an order under *subsection (2)* that—

        (*a*) the net proceeds of the disposal, and

        (*b*) where those proceeds are less than such amount as may be determined by the court to be the net amount which would be realised on a sale of the property or goods in the open market by a willing vendor, such sums as may be required to make good the deficiency.

shall be applied towards discharging the sums secured by the security or payable under the hire-purchase agreement.

(5) Where a condition imposed in pursuance of *subsection (4)* relates to two or more securities, that condition requires the net proceeds of the disposal and, where *paragraph (b)* of that subsection applies, the sums mentioned in that paragraph to be applied towards [discharging] the sums secured by those securities in the order

of their priorities.

(6) An office copy of an order under *subsection (1)* or *(2)* in relation to a security shall, within 7 days after the making of the order, be delivered by the examiner to the registrar of companies.

(7) If the examiner without reasonable excuse fails to comply with *subsection (6)*, he shall be liable to a fine not exceeding £1,000.

(8) References in this section to a hire-purchase agreement include a conditional sale agreement, a retention of title agreement and an agreement for the bailment of goods which is capable of subsisting for more than 3 months.

Notification of appointment of examiner

12.—(1) Where a petition is presented under *section 3*, notice of the petition in the prescribed form shall, within 3 days after its presentation, be delivered by the petitioner to the registrar of companies.

(2)   (*a*) An examiner shall, within the time limits specified in *paragraph (b)*, cause to be published in *Iris Oifigiúil* and in at least two daily newspapers circulating in the district in which the registered office or principal place of business of the company is situate a notice of—
            (i) his appointment and the date thereof, and
            (ii) the date, if any, set for the hearing of the matters arising out of the report to be prepared by the examiner under *section 15*.

(*b*) The time limits referred to in *paragraph (a)* are—
            (i) twenty-one days after his appointment in the case of *Iris Oifigiúil*, and
            (ii) three days after his appointment in the other case referred to in that paragraph.

(3) An examiner shall, within three days after his appointment, deliver to the registrar of companies a copy of the order appointing him.

(4) Where a company is, by virtue of *section 5*, deemed to be under the protection of the court, every invoice, order for goods or business letter issued by or on behalf of the company, being a document on or in which the name of the company appears, shall contain the statement "under the protection of the court".

(5) A person who fails to comply with the provisions of this section shall be guilty of an offence and shall be liable, on summary conviction, to a fine not exceeding £1,000 and, on conviction on indictment, to a fine not exceeding £10,000.

General provisions as to examiners

13.—(1) An examiner may resign, or on cause shown, be removed by the court.

(2) If for any reason a vacancy occurs in the office of examiner, the court may by order fill the vacancy.

(3) An application for an order under *subsection (2)* may be made by—
            (*a*) any committee of creditors established under *section 21*, or
            (*b*) the company or any interested party.

(4) An examiner shall be described by the style of "the examiner" of the particular company in respect of which he is appointed and not by his individual name.

(5) The acts of an examiner shall be valid notwithstanding any defects that may afterwards be discovered in his appointment or qualification.

(6) An examiner shall be personally liable on any contract entered into by him in the performance of his functions (whether such contract is entered into by him in the name of the company or in his own name as examiner or otherwise) unless the contract provides that he is not to be personally liable on such contract, and he shall be entitled in respect of that liability to indemnity out of the assets; but nothing in this subsection shall be taken as limiting any right to indemnity which he would have apart from this subsection, or as limiting his liability on contracts entered into without authority or as conferring any right to indemnity in respect of that liability.

(7) A company to which an examiner has been appointed or an interested party may apply to the court for the determination of any question arising out of the performance or otherwise by the examiner of his functions.

14.—(1) The directors of a company to which an examiner has been appointed shall, within 7 days of the appointment, cause to be made out, verified by affidavit and submitted to the examiner a statement in accordance with this section as to the affairs of the company. *Information to be given when examiner appointed*

(2) The statement shall, in so far as is reasonably possible to do so, show as at the date of the examiner's appointment particulars of the company's assets, debts and liabilities (including contingent and prospective liabilities), the names and addresses of its creditors, the securities held by them respectively, the dates when the securities were respectively given and such further information as may be prescribed or as the court may direct.

(3) A person to whom *subsection (1)* applies who makes default in complying with the requirements of this section shall be guilty of an offence and shall be liable, on summary conviction, to a fine not exceeding £1,000 and, on conviction on indictment, to a fine not exceeding £10,000.

15.—(1) It shall be the duty of an examiner to conduct an examination of the affairs of the company to which he is appointed and report to the court, within 21 days of his appointment or such longer period as the court may allow, the results of the examination in accordance with *section 16.* *Examination of affairs of company*

(2) Notwithstanding any other provision of this Act the court may impose on the examiner such other duties as it deems appropriate.

(3) The examiner shall deliver a copy of his report under this section to the company on the same day as his delivery of such report to the court.

(4) The examiner shall also supply a copy of his report under this section to any interested party on written application, provided that such supply may, if the court so directs, be subject to the omission of such parts of the report as the court thinks fit.

(5) The court may, in particular, give a direction under *subsection (4)* if it considers that the inclusion of certain information in the report to be supplied under that subsection would be likely to prejudice the survival of the company, or the whole or any part of its undertaking.

Examiner's
report
(amended)

16.—The examiner's report under *section 15* shall comprise the following—

(*a*) the names and permanent addresses of the officers of the company and, in so far as the examiner can establish, any person in accord- ance with whose directions or instructions the directors of the company are accustomed to act,

(*b*) the names of any other bodies corporate of which the directors of the company are also directors,

(*c*) a statement as to the affairs of the company, showing, insofar as is reasonably possible to do so, particulars of the company's assets, debts and liabilities (including contingent and prospective liabilities) as at the latest practicable date, the names and addresses of its creditors, the securities held by them respectively and the dates when the securities were respectively given,

(*d*) whether in the opinion of the examiner any deficiency between the assets and the liabilities of the company has been satisfactorily accounted for or, if not, whether there is evidence of a substantial disappearance of property that is not adequately accounted for,

(*e*) a statement of opinion by the examiner as to whether the company, and the whole or any part of its undertaking, would be capable of surivival as a going concern and a statement of the conditions which he feels are essential to ensure such survival, whether as regards the internal managament and controls of the company or otherwise,

(*f*) his opinion as to whether the formulation, acceptance and confirmation of proposals for a compromise or scheme of arrangement would facilitate such survival,

(*g*) whether, in his opinion, an attempt to continue the whole or any part of the undertaking of the company would be likely to be more advantageous to the members as a whole and the creditors as a whole, than a winding-up of the company,

(*h*) recommendations as to the course he thinks should be taken in relation to the company including, if warranted, draft proposals for a compromise or scheme of arrangement,

[(*i*) his opinion as to whether the facts disclosed would warrant further inquiries with a view to proceedings under section 297 or 297A of the Principal Act (inserted by the Companies Act, 1990), or both,]

(*j*) such other matters as the examiner thinks relevant or the court directs, and

(*k*) his opinion as to whether his work would be assisted by a direction of the court extending the role or membership of any creditors' committee referred to in *section 21*.

Hearing of
matters
arising
from
examiner's
report

17.—(1) Where, in a report made under *section 15*, the examiner expresses the opinion that—

(*a*) the whole or any part of the undertaking of the company to which he has been appointed would not be capable of survival as a going concern, or

(*b*) the formulation, acceptance, or confirmation of proposals for a compromise or scheme of arrangement wouuld not facilitate such survival, or

(*c*) an attempt to continue the whole or part of the undertaking of the company would not be likley to be more advantageous to the members as a whole, or the creditors as a whole, than a winding-up of the company, or

(*d*) there is evidence of a substantial disappearance of property that is not adequately accounted for, or of other serious irregularities in relation to the company's affairs.

the court shall, as soon as may be after the receipt of the examiner's report, hold a hearing to consider matters arising out of the report.

(2) The following parties shall be entitled to appear and be heard at a hearing under *subsection (1)*—

(*a*) the examiner,

(*b*) the company,

(*c*) any interested party,

(*d*) any person who is referred to in the report in relation to the matters mentioned in *subsection (1)(d)*.

(3) Following a hearing under this section, the court may make such order or orders as it deems fit.

(4) Without prejudice to the generality of *subsection (3)*, an order under that subsection may include any order for—

(*a*) the discharge from the protection of the court of the whole or any part of the assets of the company,

(*b*) the imposition of such terms and conditions as it sees fit for the continuance of the protection of the court,

(*c*) the winding-up of the company,

(*d*) the sale of the whole or any part of the undertaking of the company on such terms and conditions, including terms and conditions relating to the distribution of the proceeds of such sale, as the court sees fit, and, if necessary for that purpose, the appointment of a receiver,

(*e*) the formulation by the examiner of proposals for a compromise or scheme of arrangement,

(*f*) the summoning of the meetings mentioned in this Act for the purpose of considering proposals for a compromise or scheme of arrangement,

(*g*) the calling, holding and conduct of a meeting of the board of directors, or a general meeting of the company, to consider such matters as the court shall direct,

(5) On the making of an order under this section, the examiner or such other person as the court may direct shall deliver an office copy of the order to the registrar of companies for registration.

(6) Where the court makes an order for the winding-up of a company under this Act, such a winding-up shall be deemed to have commenced on the date of the making of the order, unless the court otherwise orders.

18.—(1) Where, in the opinion of the examiner—

    (*a*) the whole or any part of the undertaking of the company would be capable of survival as a going concern, and

    (*b*) an attempt to continue the whole or any part of the undertaking of the company would be likely to be more advantageous to the members as a whole, and to the creditors as a whole, than a winding-up of the company, and

    (*c*) the formulation, acceptance and confirmation of proposals for a compromise or scheme of arrangement would facilitate such survival,

the examiner shall formulate proposals for a compromise or scheme of arrangement.

(2) Notwithstanding any provision of the Companies Acts relating to notice of general meetings (but subject to notice of not less than three days in any case) the examiner shall convene and preside at such meetings of members and creditors as he thinks proper, to consider such proposals and report thereon to the court within 42 days of his appointment or such longer period as the court may allow, in accordance with *section 19*.

(3) Where, on the application of the examiner, the court is satisfied that the examiner would be unable to report to the court within the period of three months referred to in *section 5(1)* but that he would be able to make a report if that period were extended, the court may by order extend that period by not more than 30 days to enable him to do so.

(4) Where the examiner has submitted a report under this section to the court and, but for this subsection, the period mentioned in *section 5(1)* (and any extended period followed under *subsection (3)* of this section) would expire, the court may, of its own motion or on the application of the examiner, extend the period concerned by such period as the court considers necessary to enable it to take a decision under *section 24*.

(5) The examiner shall deliver a copy of his report under this section—

    (*a*) to the company on the same day as his delivery of such report to the court, and

    (*b*) to any interested party on written application,

provided that such delivery under *paragraph (b)* may, if the court so directs, be subject to the omission of such parts of the report as the court thinks fit.

(6) The court may, in particular, give a direction under *subsection (5)(b)* if it considers that the inclusion of certain information in the report to be delivered under that paragraph would be likely to prejudice the survival of the company, or the whole or any part of its undertaking.

19.—An examiner's report under section 18 shall include—

(*a*) the proposals placed before the required meetings,

(*b*) any modification of those proposals adopted at any of those meetings,

(*c*) the outcome of each of the required meetings,

(*d*) the recommendation of the committee of creditors, if any,

(*e*) a statement of the assets and liabilities (including contingent and prospective liabilities) of the company as at the date of his report,

(*f*) a list of the creditors of the company, the amount owing to each such creditor, the nature and value of any security held by any such creditor, and the priority status of any such creditor under section 285 of the Principal Act or any other statutory provision or rule of law,

(*g*) a list of the officers of the company,

(*h*) his recommendation,

(*i*) such other matters as the examiner deems appropriate or the court directs.

Examiner's report under section 18

20.—(1) Where proposals for a compromise or scheme of arrangement are to be formulated in relation to a company, the company may, subject to the approval of the court, affirm or repudiate any contract under which some element of performance other than payment remains to be rendered both by the company and the other contracting party or parties.

(2) Any person who suffers loss or damage as a result of such repudiation shall stand as an unsecured creditor for the amount of such loss or damage.

(3) In order to facilitate the formulation, consideration or confirmation of a compromise or scheme of arrangement, the court may hold a hearing and make an order determining the amount of any such loss or damage and the amount so determined shall be due by the company to the creditor as a judgement debt.

(4) Where the examiner is not a party to an application to the court for the purposes of *subsection (1)*, the company shall serve notice of such application on the examiner and the examiner may appear and be heard on the hearing of any such applicaiton.

(5) Where the court approves the affirmation or repudiation of a contract under this section, it may in giving such approval make such orders as it thinks fit for the purposes of giving full effect to its approval including orders as to notice to, or declaring the rights of, any party affected by such affirmation or repudiation.

Repudiation of certain contracts

21.—(1) An examiner may, and if so directed by the court shall, appoint a committee of creditors to assist him in the performance of his functions.

(2) Save as otherwise directed by the court, a committee appointed under *subsection (1)* shall consist of not more than five members and shall include the holders of the three largest unsecured claims who are willing to serve.

(3) The examiner shall provide the committee with a copy of any proposals for a compromise or scheme of arrangement and the committee may express an opinion on the proposals on its own behalf or on behalf of the creditors or classes of creditors

Appointment of creditors' committee

represented thereon.

(4) As soon as practicable after the appointment of a committee under *sub-section (1)* the examiner shall meet with the committee to transact such business as may be necessary.

Contents
of
proposals.

22.—(1) Proposals for a compromise or scheme of arrangement shall—

(*a*) specify each class of members and creditors of the company,

(*b*) specify any class of members and creditors whose interests or claims will not be impaired by the proposals,

(*c*) specify any class of members and creditors whose interests or claims will be impaired by the proposals,

(*d*) provide equal treatment for each claim or interest of a particular class unless the holder of a particular claim or interest agrees to less favourable treatment,

(*e*) provide for the implementation of the proposals,

(*f*) if the examiner considers it necessary or desirable to do so to facilitate the survival of the company, and the whole or any part of its undertaking, as a going concern, specify whatever changes should be made in relation to the management or direction of the company,

(*g*) if the examiner considers it necessary or desirable as aforesaid, specify any changes he considers should be made in the memorandum or articles of the company, whether as regards the management or direction of the company or otherwise,

(*h*) include such other matters as the examiner deems appropriate.

(2) A statement of the assets and liabilities (including contingent and prospective liabilities) of the company as at the date of the proposals shall be attached to each copy of the proposals to be submitted to meetings of members and creditors under *section 23*.

(3) There shall also be attached to each such copy of the proposals a description of the estimated financial outcome of a winding-up of the company for each class of members and creditors.

(4) The court may direct that the proposals include whatever other provisions it deems fit.

(5) For the purposes of this section and *sections 24* and *25*, a creditor's claim against a company is impaired if he receives less in payment of his claim than the full amount due in respect of the claim at the date of presentation of the petition for the appointment of the examiner.

(6) For the purposes of this section and *sections 24* and *25*, the interest of a member of a company in a company is impaired if—

(*a*) the nominal value of his shareholding in the company is reduced,

(*b* where he is entitled to a fixed dividend in respect of his shareholding in the company, the amount of that dividend is reduced,

(*c*) he is deprived of all or any part of the rights accruing to him by virtue of his shareholding in the company.

(*d*) his percentage interest in the total issued share capital of the company is reduced, or

(e) he is deprived of his shareholding in the company.

23.—(1) This section applies to a meeting of members or creditors or any class of members or creditors summoned to consider proposals for a compromise or scheme of arrangement.

(2) At a meeting to which this section applies a modification of the proposals may be put to the meeting but may only be accepted with the consent of the examiner.

(3) Proposals shall be deemed to have been accepted by a meeting of members or of a class of members if a majority of the votes validly cast at that meeting, whether in person or by proxy, are cast in favour of the resolution for the proposals.

(4) Proposals shall be deemed to have been accepted by a meeting of creditors or of a class of creditors when a majority in number representing a majority in value of the claims represented at that meeting have voted, either in person or by proxy, in favour of the resolution for the proposals.

(5)   (a) Where a State authority is a creditor of the company, such authority shall be entitled to accept proposals under this section notwithstanding—

(i) that any claim of such authority as a creditor would be impaired under the proposals, or

(ii) any other enactment.

(b) In this subsection, "State authority" means the State, a Minister of the Government[, a local authority] or the Revenue Commissioners.

(6) Section 144 of the Principal Act shall apply to any resolution to which *subsection (3)* or *(4)* relates which is passed at any adjourned meeting.

(7) Section 202, subsections (2) to (6), of the Principal Act shall, with the necessary modifications, apply to meetings held under this section.

(8) With every notice summoning a meeting to which this section applies which is sent to a creditor or member, there shall be sent also a statement explaining the effect of the compromise or scheme of arrangement and in particular stating any material interests of the directors of the company, whether as directors or as members or as creditors of the company or otherwise and the effect thereon of the compromise or arrangement, insofar as it is different from the effect on the like interest of other persons.

24.—(1) The report of the examiner under *section 18* shall be set down for consideration by the court as soon as may be after receipt of the report by the court.

(2) The following persons may appear and be heard at a hearing under *subsection (1)*—

(a) the company,

(b) the examiner,

(c) any creditor or member whose claim or interest would be impaired if the proposals were implemented.

(3) At a hearing under *subsection (1)* the court may, as it thinks proper, subject

*Considera-
tion by
members
and
creditors of
proposals
(amended)*

*Confirma-
tion of
proposals
(amended)*

to the provisions of this section and *section 25*, confirm, confirm subject to modifications, or refuse to confirm the proposals.

(4) The court shall not confirm any proposals—

(*a*) unless at least one class of members and one class of creditors whose interests or claims would be impaired by implementation of the proposals have accepted the proposals, or

(*b*) if the sole or primary purpose of the proposals is the avoidance of payment of tax due, or

(*c*) unless the court is satisfied that—

(i) the proposals are fair and equitable in relation to any class of members or creditors that has not accepted the proposals and whose interests or claims would be impaired by implementation, and

(ii) the proposals are not unfairly prejudicial to the interests of any interested party.

(5) Where the court confirms proposals (with or without modification), the proposals shall be binding on all the members or class or classes of members, as the case may be, affected by the proposals and also on the company.

(6) Where the court confirms proposals (with or without modification), the proposals shall, notwithstanding any other enactment, be binding on all the creditors or the class or classes of creditors, as the case may be, affected by the proposals in respect of any claim or claims against the company and any person other than the company who, under any statute, enacment, rule of law or otherwise, is liable for all or any part of the debts of the company.

(7) Any alterations in, additions to or deletions from the memorandum and articles of the company which are specified in the proposals shall, after confirmation of the proposals by the court and notwithstanding any other provisions of the Companies Acts, take effect from a date fixed by the court.

(8) Where the court confirms proposals under this section it may make such orders for the implementation of its decision as it deems fit.

(9) A compromise or scheme of arrangement, proposals for which have been confirmed under this section shall come into effect from a date fixed by the court, which date shall be not later than 21 days from the date of their confirmation.

(10) On the confirmation of proposals a copy of any order made by the court under this section shall be delivered by the examiner, or by such person as the court may direct, to the registrar of companies for registration.

(11) Where—

(*a*) the court refuses to confirm proposals under this section, or

(*b*) the report of the examiner under *section 18* concludes that, following the required meetings of members and creditors of a company under this Act, it has not been possible to reach agreement on a compromise or scheme of arrangement,

the court may, if it considers it just and equitable to do so, make an order for the winding-up of the company, or any other order as it deems fit.

[(12) Notwithstanding subsection (4), or any other provision of this Act, where the examiner forms the opinion that the company will be able to survive as a going concern, nothing in this Act shall prevent the examiner from including, in a report under *section 15* or *18*, proposals which will not involve the impairment of the interests of members or creditors of the company, nor the court from confirming any such proposals.]

25.—(1) At a hearing under *section 24* in relation to proposals a member or creditor whose interest or claim would be impaired by the proposals may object in particular to their confirmation by the court on any of the following grounds— *(Objection to confirmation by court of proposals)*

    (*a*) that there was some material irregularity at or in relation to a meeting to which *section 23* applies,

    (*b*) that acceptance of the proposals by the meeting was obtained by improper means,

    (*c*) that the proposals were put forward for an improper purpose,

    (*d*) that the proposals unfairly prejudice the interests of the objector.

(2) Any person who voted to accept the proposals may not object to their confirmation by the court except on the grounds—

    (*a*) that such acceptance was obtained by improper means, or

    (*b*) that after voting to accept the proposals he became aware that the proposals were put forward for an improper purpose.

(3) Where the court upholds an objection under this section, the court may make such order as it deems fit, including an order that the decision of any meeting be set aside and an order that any meeting be reconvened.

26.—(1) Subject to *section 5*, the protection deemed to be granted to a company under that section shall cease— *(Cessation of protection of company and termination of appointment of examiner)*

    (*a*) on the coming into effect of a compromise or scheme of arrangment under this Act, or

    (*b*) on such earlier date as the court may direct.

(2) Where a company ceases to be under the protection of the court, the appointment of the examiner shall terminate on the date of such cessation.

27.—The company or any interested party may, within 180 days after the confirmation of the proposals by the court, apply to the court for revocation of that confirmation on the grounds that it was procured by fraud and the court, if satisfied that such was the case, may revoke that confirmation on such terms and conditions, particularly with regard to the protection of the rights of parties acquiring interests or property in good faith and for value in reliance on that confirmation, as it deems fit. *(Revocation)*

28.—(1) A person shall not be qualified to be appointed or act as an examiner of a company if he would not be qualified to act as its liquidator. *(Disqualification of examiners)*

(2) A person who acts as examiner of a company while disqualified under this section shall be guilty of an offence, and shall be liable, on summary conviction,

to a fine not exceeding £1,000 and, on conviction on indictment, to a fine not exceeding £10,000.

Costs and remuneration of examiners

29.—(1) The court may from time to time make such orders as it thinks proper for payment of the remuneration and costs of, and reasonable expenses properly incurred by, an examiner.

(2) Unless the court otherwise orders, the remuneration, costs and expenses of an examiner shall be paid and the examiner shall be entitled to be indemnified in respect thereof out of the revenue of the business of the company to which he has been appointed, or the proceeds of realisation of the assets (including investments).

(3) The remuneration, costs and expenses of an examiner which have been sanctioned by order of the court shall be paid in full and shall be paid before any other claim, secured or unsecured, under any compromise or scheme of arrangement or in any receivership or winding-up of the company to which he has been appointed.

(4) The functions of an examiner may be performed by him with the assistance of persons appointed or employed by him for that purpose provided that an examiner shall, insofar as is reasonably possible, make use of the services of the staff and facilities of the company to which he has been appointed to assist him in the performance of his functions.

(5) In considering any matter relating to the costs, expenses and remuneration of an examiner the court shall have particular regard to the proviso to *subsection (4)*.

Publicity (amended)

30.—(1) An examiner or, where appropriate, such other person as the court may direct, shall, within 14 days after the delivery to the registrar of companies of every order made under *section 17* or *24*, cause to be published in *Iris Oifigiúil* notice of such delivery.

(2) Where a person fails to comply with this section, that person, and where that person is a company, the company and every officer of the company who is in default shall be guilty of an offence and shall be liable to a fine not exceeding £1,000.

Hearing of proceedings otherwise than in public

(3) . . .

31.—The whole or part of any proceedings under this Act may be heard otherwise than in public if the court, in the interests of justice, considers that the interests of the company concerned or of its creditors as a whole so require.

No lien over company's books, records etc.

[**32.**—Where the court has appointed an examiner, no person shall be entitled as against the examiner to withhold possession of any deed, instrument, or other document belonging to the company, or the books of account, receipts, bills, invoices, or other papers of a like nature relating to the accounts or trade, dealings or business of the company, or to claim any lien thereon provided that—

(*a*) where a mortgage, charge or pledge has been created by the deposit of any such document or paper with a person, the production of the document or paper to the examiner by the person shall be without prejudice to the person's rights under the mortgage or charge (other than any right to possession of the document or paper),

(*b*) where by virtue of this section an examiner has possession of any document or papers of a receiver or that a receiver is entitled to examine, the examiner shall, unless the court otherwise orders, make the document or papers available for inspection by the receiver at all reasonable times

33.—(1) If in the course of proceedings under this Act it appears that—

Civil liability of persons concerned for fraudulent trading of company

(*a*) any person was, while an officer of the company, knowingly a party to the carrying on of any business of the commpany in a reckless manner; or

(*b*) any peson who knowingly a party to the carrying on of any business of the company with intent to defraud creditors of the company, or creditors of any other person or for any fraudulent purpose;

the court, on the application of the examiner, or any creditor or contributory of the company, may, if it thinks it proper to do so, declare that such person shall be personally responsible, without any limitation of liability, for all or any part of the debts or other liabilities of the company as the court may direct.

(2) Without prejudice to the generality of *subsection (1)(a)*, an officer of the company shall be deemed to ahve been knowingly a party to the carrying on of any business of the company in a reckless manner if—

(*a*) he was a party to the carrying on of such business and, having regard to the general knowledge, skill and experience that may reasonably be expected of a person in his position, he ought to have known that his actions or those of the company would cause loss to the creditors of the company, or any of them, or

(*b*) he was a party to the contracting of a debt by the company and did not honestly believe on reasonable grounds that the company would be abel to pay the debt when it fell due for payment as well as all its other debts (taking into account the contingent and prospective liabilities).

(3) Notwithstanding anything contained in *subsection (1)* the court may grant a declaration on the grounds set out in *paragraph (a)* of the subsection only if—

(*a*) paragraph (a), (b) or (c) of section 214 of the Principal Act applies to the company concerned, and

(*b*) an applicant for such a declaration, being a creditor or contributory of the company, or any person on whose behalf such application is made, suffered loss or damage as a consequence of any behaviour mentioned in *subsection (1)*.

(4) In deciding whether it is proper to make an order on the ground set out in *subesection (2)(b)*, the court shall have regard to whether the creditor in question was, at the time the debt was incurred, aware of the company's financial state of affairs and, notwithstanding such awareness, nevertheless assented to the incurring

of the debt.

(5) On the hearing of an application under this section, the applicant may himself give evidence or call witnesses.

(6) Where it appears to the court that any person in respect of whom a declaration has been sought under *subsection (1)(a)* has acted honestly and responsibly in relation to the conduct of the affairs of the company or any matter or matters on the ground of which such declaration is sought to be made, the court may, having regard to all the circumstances of the case, relieve him either wholly or in part, from personal liability on such terms as it may think fit.

(7) Where the court makes any such declaration, it may—

(*a*) give such further directions as it thinks proper for the purpose of giving effect to the declaration and in particular make provision for making the liability of any such person under the declaration a change on any debt or obligation due from the company to him, or on any mortgage or charge or any interest in any mortgage or charge on any assets of the company held by or vested in him or any company or person on his behalf, or any person claiming an assignee from or through the person liable or any company or person acting on his behalf, and may from time to time make such further orders as may be necessary for the purpose of enforcing any charge imposed under this subsection;

(*b*) provide that such sums recovered under this section shall be paid to such person or classes of persons, for such purposes, in such amounts or proportions at such time or times and in such respective priorities among themselves as such declaration may specify.

(8) This section shall have effect notwithstanding that—

(*a*) the person in respect of whom the declaration has been sought under *subsection (1)* may be criminally liable in respect of the matters on the ground of which such declaration is to be made; or

(*b*) any matter or matters on the ground of which the declaration under *subsection (1)* is to be made have occurred outside the State.

(9) *Subsection (1)(a)* shall not apply during a period when the company is under the protection of the court.

(10) For the purpose of this section—

"assignee" includes any person to whom or in whose favour, by the directions of the person liable, the debt, obligation, mortgage or charge was created, issued or transferred or the interest created, but does not include an assignee for valuable consideration (not including consideration by way of marriage) given in good faith and without notice of any of the matters on the grounds of which the declaration is made;

"company" includes any body which may be wound up under the Companies Acts; and

"officer" includes any auditor, liquidator, receiver, or any person in accordance with whose directions or instructions the directors of the company are accustomed to act.

34.—(1) If any person is knowingly a party to the carrying on of the business of the company with intent to defraud creditors of the company or creditors of any other person or for any fraudulent purpose, that person shall be guilty of an offence.

(2) Any person who is convicted of an offence under this section shall be liable—

(*a*) on sumary conviction, to imprisonment for a term not exceeding 12 months or to a fine not exceeding £1,000 or to both, or

(*b*) on conviction on indictment, to imprisonment for a term not exceeding 7 months or to a fine not exceeding £50,000 or to both.

Criminal liability of persons concerned for fraudulent trading of company

35.—(1) Where, on the application of an examiner of a company, it can be shown to the satisfaction of the court that—

(*a*) any property of the company of any kind whatsoever was disposed of either by way of conveyance, transfer, mortgage, security, loan, or in any way whatsoever whether by act or omission, direct or indirect, and

(*b*) the effect of such disposal was to perpetrate a fraud on the company, its creditors or members,

the court may, if it deems it just and equitable to do so, order any person who appears to have the use, control or possession of such property or the proceeds of the sale or development thereof to deliver it or pay a sum in respect of it to the examiner on such terms or conditions as the court sees fit.

(2) *Subsection (1)* shall not apply to any conveyance, mortgage, delivery of goods, payment, execution or other act relating to property made or done by or against a company to which section 286(1) of the Principal Act applies.

(3) In deciding whether it is just and equitable to make an order under this section, the court shall have regard to the rights of persons who have bona fide and for value acquired an interest in the property the subject of the application.]

Power of court to order the return of assets which have been improperly transferred

36.—(1) Any order made by a court of any country recognised for the purposes of this section and made for or in the course of the reorganisation or reconstruction of a company may be enforced by the High Court in all respects as if the order had been made by the High Court.

(2) When an application is made to the High Court under this section, an office copy of any order sought to be enforced shall be sufficient evidence of the order.

(3) In this section, "company" means a body corporate incorporated outside the State, and "recognised" means recognised by order made by the Minister.

Enforce-ment of reconstruc-tion orders made by courts outside the State

[**36A.**—Proceedings in relation to an offence under section 11(6), 12 or 30 may be brought and prosecuted by the registrar of companies.]

Proceed-ings by registrar

37.—(1) This Act may be cited as the Companies (Amendment) Act, 1990.

(2) This Act and the Companies Acts, 1963 to 1986, may be cited together as the Companies Acts, 1963 to 1990.

(3) The Companies Acts, 1963 to 1986, and this Act shall be construed together as one Act.

Short title, collective citation and constructio

APPENDIX II

Rules of the Superior Courts

Order 75A
Proceedings under the Companies (Amendment) Act 1990 (No. 27 of 1990)

1.—In this Order, unless the context or subject matter otherwise requires—

(1) "The Act" means the Companies (Amendment) Act 1990 (No. 27 of 1990).

(2) Words and expressions contained in this Order shall have the same meaning as in the Act and where necessary the same meaning as in the Companies Acts 1963-1990.

(3) "The 1986 Rules" means the Rules of the Superior Courts S.I. No. 15 of 1986.

(4) "The Examiner" shall include the Interim Examiner.

2.—All applications and proceedings for or in relation to an appointment of an Examiner under the Act or concerning such examination shall be be assigned to such Judge of Judges as the President of the High Court shall from time to time assign to hear such applications and proceedings, but if such Judge or Judges shall be unable to dispose of such applications or proceedings, any other Judge or Judges of the High Court may dispose of any such application.

3.—An application under section 2 of the Act shall be grounded on the petition and the affidavit of the party making such application and shall be heard and determined on affidavit unless the Court otherwise orders.

4.—(1) A petition for the appointment of an Examiner under the Act shall be presented at and shall be retained in the Central Office. A sealed copy thereof shall be taken out by the petitioner or by his solicitor and shall be used as if it were an original.

(2) The petition shall be brought to the office of one of the registrars who shall appoint the time and place at which the petition is to be heard.

(3) Every petition for the appointment of an Examiner shall be verified by affidavit. Such affidavit shall be made by the petitioner or by one of the petitioners if more than one, or in case the petition is presented by a corporation or company, by one of the directors, secretary or other officer thereof and shall be sworn before the presentation of the petition and filed with such petition and such affidavit shall

be sufficient *prima facie* evidence of the statements in the petition. The form of the petition shall comply with section 3(3) of the Act and shall also, so far as applicable, comply with Form No. 2 in Appendix M of the 1986 rules.

(4) On the same day as the petition shall have been presented, the petitioner shall apply *ex parte* to the High Court for directions as to proceedings to be taken in relation thereto.

5.—(1) On the hearing of the *ex parte* application referred to in Rule 4(4) above or on any adjourned hearing or hearings thereof or on any subsequent application, the Court may make such order or orders as it thinks fit and may give such directions as it thinks fit and in particular may give directions as to the parties on whom the petition should be served, the mode of service, the time for such service, the date for the hearing of the petition (if different to that appointed by the Registrar) and whether the said petition should be advertised and if so, how the same should be advertised.

(2) On the hearing of such *ex parte* application, the Court may, if it thinks fit, treat the application as the hearing of the petition and may make such interim order or any other order it thinks fit including adjourning the hearing and may appoint any proposed Examiner on an interim basis until such adjourned hearing and an Examiner so appointed over any company or any related company shall be referred to as the Interim Examiner and shall have the same powers and duties in relation to such company until the date of the adjourned hearing as if he were an Examiner appointed other than on an interim basis.

(3) The Court may adjourn the hearing of the petition or any adjourned hearing until any party or parties which the Court considers should be notified have been notified of the presentation of the petition, whether by advertisement or otherwise, and may adjourn any hearing of the petition for any other reason that appears to the Court to be just and equitable.

(4) On the hearing of a petition or on the adjournment or the further hearing of such petition, the Court may, having heard the petitioner and any interested party or any person who has been notified of the petition and who appears thereto, as the case may be, appoint an Examiner, and may make such further or other order as it thinks fit.

6.—(1) An application for the appointment of an Examiner to be appointed an Examiner of a related company pursuant to section 4 of the Act if brought by the petitioner or by the Examiner shall be made *ex parte* to the Court provided that on the hearing of any such application, the Court may make such order or orders or give such directions as it thinks fit including directions as to whether, and if so, upon which parties notice of the application should be served, the mode of such service and time allowed for such service and whether the application should be advertised and if so, how the same should be advertised and may adjourn the hearing of such application to a date to be specified.

(2) The Court may, if it thinks fit, while adjourning such application, make such interim order as it sees fit including the appointment of the Examiner as the

Examiner of the related company on an intrerim basis and may also confer on such Examiner in relation to such company all or any of the powers and duties conferred on him in relation to the first mentioned company on an interim basis until the adjourned hearing.

(3) An application for the appointment of an Examiner to be the Examiner of a related company shall, if brought by any person other than the petitioner or the Examiner of the first mentioned company, be brought by way of notice of motion served upon the Examiner and petitioner.

7.—In any case where an Interim Examiner has been appointed to any company or an Examiner has been appointed Interim Examiner of a related company of that company, and where upon the final hearing of the application or of the petition, as the case may be, no Examiner is appointed to that company or to that related company, as the case may be, or where a person other than the Interim Examiner is appointed as Examiner to the company or to the related company, such Interim Examiner shall prepare a written report for the Court in relation to the company or to the related company or both in such time as the Court shall direct. Such report or reports shall as far as possible in the circumstances deal with the matters specified in section 16(a) to (1) of the Act. Such Examiner shall keep and maintain a true record of all liabilities certified by him under section 10 of the Act and shall in his written report give a full account of all liabilities so certified to the Court and shall deal with such further or other matters as may be directed by the Court.

8.—(1) Any application by an Examiner of a company pursuant to section 5(3) of the Act in relation to any existing proceedings involving that company shall be brought by motion on notice to all the parties to such proceedings including the company in relation to which the Examiner was appointed.

(2) Any application by any person under section 5(3) of the Act seeking the leave of the Court to commence proceedings in relation to the company shall be brought by way of motion on notice to the Examiner and to the company.

9.—(1) Any application by any Examiner pursuant to section 7(6) of the Act may be made *ex parte* to the Court and on hearing of any such application the Court may deal with the application and may make such order or orders in relation thereto as it thinks fit or may adjourn the application and give such directions as to proceedings to be taken upon it as it thinks fit.

(2) Any application, by any member, contributory, creditor or director of a company pursuant to section 7(6) of the Act shall be by way of motion on notice to the Examiner and to the company and the Court may make such order upon such application as if it had been brought by the Examiner.

(3) An application by the company or by an interested party pursuant to section 13(7) of the Act shall be made by motion on notice to the Examiner and to any other interested party or the company, as the case may be, and the Court may deal with any such application as if it were an application under section 7(6) of the Act and make such order as appears just and proper in the circumstances.

10.—Once an examiner has certified any refusal or refusals specified in section 8(5) of the Act, he shall thereupon apply *ex parte* to the Court for leave to produce the said Certificate in relation to such refusal and shall verify the facts in the Certificate by affidavit and thereupon the Court upon notice to the party concerned, may make such enquiries and give such directions in relation to the said refusals as it thinks fit and shall hear such evidence as may be produced in relation thereto and may make such order as seems just and proper in the circumstances.

11.—Any application to the Court by the Examiner pursuant to section 9 of the Act for the further vesting in him of all or any of the powers or functions vested in or exercisable by the directors of the company shall be made by notice of motion served upon the said directors, grounded on the affidavit of the Examiner specifying which, if not all, of the powers he seeks to have vested in him by Order of the Court and the Court may give such directions in relation to the hearing of the said application as it thinks fit.

12.—An application by the Examiner, pursuant to section 11 of the Act for the disposal of any property which is the subject of any security or of any goods which are in the possession of the company under a hire purchase agreement, shall be made by notice of motion grounded upon affidavit of the Examiner and served upon the holder of such security or the hire purchase company, as the case may be, or upon any other person who appears to have an interest in the property and the Court may upon the hearing of the application make such order under section 11 as appears just and proper and may give such directions concerning the proceeds of all such disposals as shall have been authorised by the Court.

13.—An Examiner wishing to resign pursuant to section 13 of the Act, shall do so by an application *ex parte* to the Court. On the hearing of the application the Court may, if it thinks fit, direct that notice of the application be served on the petitioner, the company, the directors of the company or any other interested party as may be appropriate. The application of the Examiner shall be grounded upon an affidavit sworn by him, specifying the reasons for the said proposed resignation, and the date of the said proposed resignation. Upon the application, the Court may make such order as appears just and proper in the circumstances.

(2) An application to the Court pursuant to section 13 of the Act to remove an Examiner shall be made by motion on notice to the Examiner, to the petitioner, to the company and its directors and to any other party as the Court may direct. Such application shall be grounded upon an affidavit of the moving party specifying the cause alleged to exist justifying the removal of the Examiner by the Court. On the hearing of the application, the Court may make such order as appears just in the circumstances and, if satisfied that cause has been shown for the removal of the Examiner by the Court shall order that he be removed forthwith or upon such date as the Court shall specify. The Court may either before or after ruling upon the application for the removal of the Examiner make such order for the production of

any document of documents, or the preparation of such report or reports as it thinks fit.

(3) An application pursuant to section 13(2) of the Act to fill a vacancy in the office of an Examiner shall be made *ex parte* to the Court provided that the Court may, if it thinks fit, adjourn the application and make such order or give such directions as appear proper in the circumstances, including directions for service of notice of the making of an application upon such party as it thinks proper.

14.—When an Examiner has prepared a report of his examination of the company within the time prescribed or within such time as shall have been fixed by the Court, he shall effect delivery of his report under section 15 of the Act, by making an *ex parte* application to the Court for leave to deliver it. The report shall contain a part in which each of the matters specified in section 16 shall be dealt with in the order set out in the section. The Examiner shall verify by affidavit:

    (*a*) Whether the petitioner has complied with section 12(1) of the Act.

    (*b*) Whether he has complied with section 12(2) and (3) of the Act.

    (*c*) Whether and what portions of the report (if any) should be omitted from delivery under section 15.

He shall also draw to the attention of the Court any particular aspects of the report which are or may be relevant to the exercise by the Court of any other of its functions under the Act.

15.—On application for liberty to deliver a report under section 15 of the Act, and where it appears to the Court by reason of all or any of the matters specified in section 17(1) of the Act that a hearing is required to consider matters arising out of the report, the Court shall give such directions for the holding of a hearing to consider matters arising therefrom and shall make an order fixing the date of the hearing and an order directing the service of a notice of motion for the date of the hearing upon any party entitled to appear and be heard at such hearing, and upon such other party as the Court may direct and the Court may give directions as to the mode of service of such motion on any party or parties and may give directions as to whether, and if so, how the hearing for the consideration of the report should be advertised, and the Court may make such other order or orders as it deems fit.

16.—When an examiner has been given leave to deliver his report under section 15 and where the Examiner is formulating proposals pursuant to section 18 of the Act for a compromise or scheme of arrangement, any application for an extension of time for the delivery by the Examiner of his report thereon, shall be made *ex parte* to the Court within the time for the delivery of the report or as extended by the Court. Any party affected by the extension, may on notice of motion to the Examiner apply to the Court to set the said order aside upon grounds to be specified and verified in an affidavit and on such application, the Court may make such orders it thinks fit.

17.—When an Examiner has prepared a report pursuant to section 18 of the Act within the time prescribed or within such time as shall have been fixed by the Court, he shall effect delivery of his report by making an *ex parte* application to the Court to deliver it.

(2) (*a*) The report shall contain a full account of each meeting convened by the Examiner and of the proposals put before each such meeting and shall contain as an appendix to the said report a copy of the said proposals which shall deal with each of the matters specified in section 22 of the Act in the order set out in that section.

(*b*) The Examiner shall in his application specify whether and if so, what portions of the report should be omitted from delivery under section 18(5) of the Act and he shall draw to the attention of the Court any particular aspects of the report which are or may be relevant to the exercise by the Court of any other of its functions under the Act.

(3) When the Examiner has been given leave to deliver his report pursuant to subrule 1 and where the Examiner has formulated proposals pursuant to section 18 of the Act for a compromise or scheme of arrangement and has reported to the Court thereon in the period prescribed or within such further period as may have been specified by the Court, the Examiner may apply to the Court *ex parte* for an extension of the period for protection pursuant to section 18(4) of the Act for such further period as may be necessary for the Court to enable it to take a decision in relation to the report of the Examiner on the proposals. Upon the making of the application, the Court may direct that the Examiner serve notice of the application on such party or parties as the Court thinks fit. The Court may adjourn the application to enable the service to take place, but may extend the period concerned until the adjourned date of the hearing or such other date as to the Court may seem fit, and the Court may further extend the period concerned in the event of any further adjournments of the said hearing.

18.—All meetings of members or classes of members or creditors or classes of creditors convened for the purposes of section 18 or section 23 of the Act shall be governed by the following rules:

(1) The Examiner shall summon all meetings of creditors and members by sending by post not less than 3 days before the day appointed for the meeting to every person appearing in the company's books to be a creditor of the company or a member of the company, notice of the meeting of creditors or members as the case may be.

(2) The notice to each creditor or member shall be sent to the address given in the report of the Examiner of the company, if any or to such other address as may be known to the Examiner.

(3) An affidavit by the Examiner or solicitor or by some other officer or clerk of the company or its solicitors that the notice of any meeting has been duly posted shall be suffiicent evidence of such notice having been duly sent to the person to whom the same was addressed. The Examiner may fix a meeting or meetings to be held at such place as in his opinion is most convenient for the majority of creditors

or members, or both and different times and/or places may be named for the meetings of creditors and members.

(4) The Examiner shall preside at and be chairman of any meeting which he has convened and shall conduct the business of the meeting in an orderly manner so as to ensure the proper discussion of all proposals placed by him before the said meeting.

(5) Where a meeting of creditors or members is summoned by notice, the proceedings and resolutions of the meeting shall unless the Court otherwise orders be valid, notwithstanding that some creditors or members may not have received the notice sent to them.

(6) The Examiner may with the consent of the meeting adjourn from time to time and from place to place but the adjourned meeting shall be held at the same place as the original meeting unless in the resolution for adjournment another place is specified or unless the Court otherwise orders.

(7)   (a) A meeting may not act for any purpose except the adjournment of the meeting unless there are present or represented thereat in the case of a creditors' meeting, at least 3 creditors ruled by the Examiner to be entitled to vote or in the case of a meeting of members, at least 2 members.

(b) If within 15 minutes from the time appointed by the meeting, a quorum of creditors or members as the case may be is not present or represented, the meeting shall be adjourned for the same day in the following week at the same time and place or to such other day or time or place as the Examiner may appoint but so that the day appointed shall be not less than 3, nor more than 21 days from the date from which the meeting was adjourned.

(8)   (a) The Examiner shall cause minutes of the proceedings of the meeting to be drawn up and entered in a book kept for that purpose and the minutes shall be signed by him.

(b) The Examiner shall cause a list of creditors or members present at every meeting to be kept and every such list shall be signed by him.

(9) A creditor or member may appear either in person or by proxy. Where a person is authorised in the manner provided by section 139 of the Companies Act 1963 to represent a corporation at any meeting of creditors or members, such person shall produce to the Examiner a copy of the resolution so authorising him. Such copies shall be under the seal of the corporation or be certified to be a true copy by the secretary or director of the corporation.

(10) Every instrument of proxy shall be, as far as possible, in either the Form No. 21 or Form No. 22 of Appendix M of the 1986 Rules.

(11) A general and a special form of proxy shall be sent to each of the creditors or members with a notice summoning the meeting and neither the name nor the description of the Examiner or any other person shall be printed or inserted in the body of any instrument of proxy before it is sent.

(12) A creditor or a member may appoint any person a special proxy to vote at any specified meeting or adjournment thereof on all questions relating to any matter

arising at the meeting or an adjournment thereof.

(13) A creditor or member may appoint the Examiner to act as his general or special proxy.

(14) (a) Every instrument of proxy shall be lodged with the Examiner no later than 4.00 in the afternoon of the day before the meeting or adjourned meeting at which it is to be used and the same shall be kept by the Examiner.

(b) No person who is an infant shall be appointed a general or special proxy.

(c) Where a company is a creditor, any person who is duly authorised under the seal of such company to act, generally on behalf of the company at meetings of creditors and members, may fill in and sign the instrument of proxy on such company's behalf and appoint himself to be such company's proxy and the instrument of proxy so filled in and signed by such person shall be received and dealt with as a proxy of such company.

(15) The Examiner shall have power to allow or disallow the vote of a person claiming to be a creditor or member, if he thinks fit, but his decision may be subject to appeal to the Court. If he is in doubt whether a vote should be allowed or disallowed, he shall allow it and record the vote as such subject to the vote being declared invalid in the event of an objection being taken and sustained by the Court.

19.—An application by the company pursuant to section 20 of the Act to repudiate any contract or any application arising out of such repudiation shall be made by motion on notice to the Examiner and on notice to the other contracting party or parties and on notice to any person referred to in section 20(2) of the Act.

20.—When on the consideration of a report under section 17 or under section 24, the Court considers that an order for the winding-up of the company should be made, the Court may order that the application for the winding-up of the company or of any related company be made by the Examiner or by such other person as the court may direct and the court may order that the provisions of Order 74 of the 1986 Rules, either in whole or in part, shall apply to the winding-up as ordered by the Court.

21.—(1) An application to the Court pursuant to section 27 of the Act for the revocation of confirmation of proposals confirmed by the Court, shall be made *ex parte* for directions as to the proceedings to be taken and the application shall be grounded upon an affidavit which shall specify the fraud alleged and shall supply full particulars thereof and shall specify the names and addresses of all parties who have or may have acquired interests or property in good faith and for value and in reliance on the confirmation of the proposals by the Court.

(2) Upon such application, the Court may make such order and give such directions for the hearing of the said application including directions for service of notice of the application upon all such parties as appear proper in the circumstances and may give such further directions as to the application, including particularly,

whether and if so, how the same should be advertised and if it seems fit, direct the filing of any pleadings in the matter.

22.—An application by the Examiner pursuant to section 29 of the Act for payment to him of remuneration and costs and reasonable expenses properly incurred by him shall be made by application *ex parte* to the Court and upon an affidavit of the Examiner in which he shall set forth a full account of the work carried out by him to the date of the application and a full account of the costs and expenses incurred by him and shall vouch same and of the basis for the proposed remuneration which he is seeking to be paid. The Court may, where it thinks fit, order that notice of the application be given to all such persons as the Court may direct, and may give directions as to the service of the said notice and fix a date for the hearing of the application of the Examiner. The affidavit of the Examiner shall also specify what use, if any, he has made of the services of the staff and/or of the facilities of the company to which he has been appointed and the extent of such use.

23.—An application to the Court pursuant to section 33 of the Act shall be made by motion on notice to the person or persons concerned and the provisions of Order 74 Rule 49 of the 1986 Rules shall apply to such application as if the references therein to sections of the Companies Act 1963 was a reference to section 33 of the Act.

24.—An application by the Examiner to the Court pursuant to section 35 of the Act in respect of any property of a company alleged to have been improperly transferred to the use, control or possession of any person shall be made by motion on notice to such person and the provisions of Order 74 Rule 49 of the 1986 Rules shall apply to such applications as if the references therein to sections of the Companies Act 1963 was a reference to section 35 of the Act.

2. These Rules shall be construed together with the Rules of the Superior Courts.

3. These Rules shall come into operation on the 17 day of June, 1991.

Explanatory Note

(This is not part of the Instrument and does not purport to be a legal interpretation thereof)

This instrument makes Rules governing procedures to take account of the provisions of the Companies (Amendment) Act (No. 27 of 1990).

Subject Index